THE CHANGE INTELLIGENCE FACTOR

Mastering the Promise of EXTRA-ORDINARY

JANE R. FLAGELLO

TPH
Trainers Publishing House
Fairfax, Virginia

Trainers Publishing House
www.trainerspublishinghouse.com
Email: info@trainerspublishinghouse.com

Ordering Information

Quantity Sales: sales@trainerspublishinghouse.com
Individual Sales: Amazon.com and Kindle.com

Library of Congress Control Number: 2013945202
ISBN 13: 978-1-939247-02-5 (Print)
ISBN 13: 978-1-939247-03-2 (Kindle)

TPH Editorial Team:

Publisher/Editor: Cat Russo
Editorial Manager: Jacqueline Edlund-Braun
Rights Associate and Data Manager: Nancy Silva
Communication Specialist: Stephanie Sussan
Design and Composition: Debra Deysher, Double D Media
Marketing: Dawn Baron, Passion Profits Consulting

Cover and text design by Debra Deysher
Cover art: Butrek, Shutterstock

Contents

Change Intelligence Factor Defined

The change intelligence factor is your capacity to interpret your experiences in self-affirming terms, empowering you to dance with the daily change challenges that life presents. The underlying goal is to learn and incorporate practices that enable you to develop into someone who lives with dignity, generosity, and integrity, someone who offers positive contributions to society, and someone who embraces life fully—in short, someone extra-ordinary.

Preface: The Idea of Mastery

You are the first organization you must master.
—Stuart Heller

Behind the idea of mastery lives an invitation to choose your own destiny. Between your birth and your death, many opportunities to grow present themselves, usually disguised as seemingly insurmountable problems or challenges. And while many people shy away, thinking themselves unable or unworthy, embracing mastery allows you to see each challenge for what it is—an opportunity to grow, develop, mature, and reach your full potential.

To start you must accept that there is more to your life than working 9 to 5 and accumulating stuff. You must believe that everything is possible for you. Nothing is preordained about who you are and what you can achieve. While not everyone can be a superstar basketball player, concert pianist, or brain surgeon, everyone is born with gifts. Uncovering your natural talents and using them in productive ways places you on a rich and rewarding path, even when it sometimes challenges you to your very soul.

Once you commit to your own growth and development, you can embark on a learning journey that personifies freedom. You assess where you are now and where you have decided you want to be. You harness your courage and accept your vulnerability. You take those tentative first steps that always accompany the new and unfamiliar, experiment, and take prudent risks in order to grow. Reflecting on your outcome, you intensify those actions that hone your talents and abilities and propel you closer to your chosen goals. When you falter, and you will, you pick yourself up, reassess, adjust, and act anew. You persist. You keep what works and let go of what doesn't. You pay attention to your emotions and the physical signals your body sends, thus strengthening both your emotional and physical core. You emerge stronger and more capable with each passing day.

Your life is a work in progress. When your actions and decisions build on a solid foundation that honors the principles and personal beliefs you hold dear, you advance along the change intelligence factor continuum. As you embody new learning, such as the practices and applications I share with you in this book, that mastery eases your path, until the next challenge presents itself. I encourage you to welcome your challenges with open arms. Each one holds insights about who you are and, more important, who you can become—someone extra-ordinary.

The end is where we start from.
—*T. S. Eliot*

Introduction: Designing the Alliance

Nobody goes to work to do a bad job.
—W. Edwards Deming

Change or die! Dramatic rhetoric, maybe, but the facts are clear. The ability to change is the single most important critical success factor that separates successful people and the organizations they serve from those that flounder and struggle.

People don't suffer change easily—for good reason. Change takes you out of your comfort zone. It can be frightening and confusing, leaving you feeling vulnerable. Change is a shoe that pinches. If embracing change in turbulent times is the holy grail of what it takes to be successful now, then the number one imperative, your ability to change, is on trial every day. The bottom line, mastering change, is your only real personal competitive advantage. The change intelligence factor is all about learning how to master change.

Control is an illusion. After a short time on the job, the reality sets in for most employees, managers, and leaders that there are simply too many moving parts to expect to control anything. The most intricate and promising strategic plans are always at the mercy of the people executing them, the policies and procedures in place, unpredictable customers, or innumerable unseen forces. A late delivery of a critical part, a call from an angry customer, an incorrect product installation, or a disgruntled employee can all wreak havoc with the most brilliant strategy. Couple this list with the complexity of an unpredictable economic climate and increasing costly government regulations, and the challenges businesses face grow exponentially.

Many new business models have been proposed to replace command-and-control hierarchies, but few have actually secured a solid footing in most organizations. And while asking the "why" question seems obvious, the answers offer few workable solutions. The chasm between expectations (what we want) and reality (what we get) appears too great. The shift from demands and obligations to contributions and service seems too big. Organizations don't know how to change what they are doing to produce what they claim to want.

Employees also need to think more carefully about what type of workplace best fits their needs. Navigating the ups and downs of the turbulent economy, aligning skill sets with current jobs and those yet to be designed for the future, wanting meaningful work and a life outside of work all take on new importance when so many decisions seem out of their control. While the highly educated, talented few will always have options, the majority of employees continue to feel alienated from their work and the organizations employing them, and they are fearful that their work might be taken away from them without much notice. This does not bode well when we need all hands on deck to restore America to a robust, growing economy.

Something needs to change. To begin to grapple with the complexities of the current workplace, consider this question:

> If we reconstitute employment as a mutually beneficial, designed alliance between two willing parties—an employer and an employee—how might this distinction change your perception of your role in the organization and your responsibilities?

Contemplating this question exposes the unraveling of the relationship and expectations between employers and employees. There is now much less loyalty on both sides of the employment equation. A new frame is needed to reconstitute this fraying relationship. To be successful today, you need fresh insights and distinctions regarding the effort-to-outcome equation: what work means and the role any organization plays in your life. And more than just fresh thinking, you need to know how to operationalize your efforts to create the outcomes you want, as an organization and as an individual employee. What are the strategies and tools that will enable everyone's best performance?

To get your creative juices flowing vis-à-vis both the twenty-first century organization and the changing roles of all employees, consider a Seurat painting. Seen from a distance, it's a complete visual scene. Get close and you may be surprised to see that the painting is really composed of thousands of individual colored dots. Together, the dots play in synchronistic harmony, and voilá, a masterpiece is created.

Now apply this metaphor to the world of organizations. From a distance, business operations flow through processes designed to achieve established goals. When everything works and the goals are achieved, it can appear almost effortless, a masterpiece of people and processes in synchronistic harmony. However, when some aspect of this relationship between work and people is missing or off kilter, the output suffers and so do the people involved.

Keep going. If you think of yourself as one of these thousands of dots, can you see how your efforts fit into the larger picture? What if your dot spreads into more of a slash, how does that change the picture? What if your dot expands in ways that blur the image? What if your dot grows too large in relation to surrounding dots? Or too small? What if your dot goes missing?

As the world changes, so must organizations and the people within them. The shift from command and control to more collaborative, motivating, and innovative environments has inherent costs. Participating in these more flexible and freeing communities requires a different framing narrative, a different skill set from all employees. And the most important skill, if it can even be called a skill, is your ability to change. Once you choose to become truly successful in all aspects of your life, learning to dance with change as it shows up minute by minute, being completely accountable for your actions, and becoming self-generating (able to initiate actions that will foster success for you and others) are your price of admission.

But beware! While change exerts a powerful force, the status quo is an equally powerful, often unrecognized, force. It lulls you into a false sense of complacency. It's the "bird-in-hand" expression come to life. Why chance changing anything? Fears of loss and an increased sense of vulnerability tend to reinforce the status quo. You know what your current actions are producing. You know how to compensate in those areas not fully up to speed. In some way, you have made a conscious or unconscious decision that you can live with this outcome (the devil you know).

> *Your life does not get better by chance,*
> *it gets better by change.*
> *—Jim Rohn*

The Change Intelligence Factor: Mastering the Promise of Extra-Ordinary marries emotional intelligence research to your individual ability to change. And change is all about emotions. To let go of what you have always done or planned to do and then to seek new ways to accomplish your goals is an emotional experience that plays out cognitively, emotionally, and physically.

Research has shown that learning about emotional intelligence is very important to both your personal and professional success

(Goleman 1998). The five competencies of emotional intelligence (self-awareness, self-regulation, motivation, empathy, and social skills) establish a platform that can lead to increases in performance and productivity. Your ability to recognize and monitor your own emotional currents and those of others and then use this information to guide your actions can produce better results. Although some might argue that discussing emotions in the workplace is verboten or, at the very least, dangerous, I believe that emotions are the fuel for action. They exist just below the surface in every person and organization. Learning how to use emotional energy in ways that support desired outcomes offers a tremendous payoff to you and your organization.

What's missing in all of the discussions about change is the important internal piece—what's going on inside you that causes you to do what you do—and how to change yourself (meaning grow and develop) in ways that endure. Stripped to its core, change intelligence is all about how you learn and then embody that learning to become your best.

Enter the change intelligence factor. The factor includes three personal practices that reframe your emotional structures from the inside out thus building your capacity to change. In this context, the word *change* means growth, development, transformation. Change intelligence touches your emotional chords. As your inner understanding grows, you learn how to embody a more authentic and human version of yourself, which in turn facilitates intimacy, trust, and a higher quality of life. Incorporating the three change intelligence factor practices allows you to become the instrument of your own success. The stronger your change intelligence factor becomes, the easier it is for you to successfully meet the challenges of a dynamic and complex environment. The weaker your change intelligence factor, the more you struggle to cope with seemingly insurmountable obstacles.

Change must become your mantra.

All change is personal first, public second. Change initiatives must connect at an individual, private place. The behaviors, attitude, and actions must touch you internally. From here, change initiatives translate into effective visible actions in the public arena. When this connection is missing or tenuous, change initiatives falter and fail. To achieve this private-to-public shift requires change to be understood differently. Consider the following three points that I believe to be true of today's workplace:

- Organizational change is the culmination of each individual changing and then working in concert to create a mutually desired outcome.

- Individual efforts and personal performances drive a winning business dynamic.

- Maximizing the capabilities of each individual around change is the real challenge all organizations face.

The third point is the essence of the change intelligence factor. By developing and strengthening your change intelligence skills, you can change your results. You can make choices that are more aligned with the work you want to do and the life you want to live. This journey begins by examining the practices currently fueling your interactions with people and your approaches to problems— your perceptions, emotions, and relationships, and the actions born from them. The journey continues by harnessing the power behind various combinations of these practices, keeping the mix that enables the results you really want and letting go of the behaviors that prove detrimental to your success. To authentically make these internal behavior shifts, you must hone your ability to change, allowing change to work for you, not against you.

Change is the process by which
the future invades our lives.
—Alvin Toffler

I have structured this book around three discussions (chapters) that will show you how to develop your capacity to change (that is, your change intelligence). The first discussion examines how change works at a personal level and equips you to embrace change initiatives as they are introduced. The second discussion shares three critical change practices that are the backbone behaviors you need to develop. The third discussion explores the public domain, your organization where the dynamics of change play out through the relationships among co-workers, customers, and clients every day. I offer you four powerful applications to enable you to create a high-performing, engaging organization. In the final chapter, I encourage you to embrace personal trans-formation, as if you were a coaching client in my office.

Self-discipline through self-awareness, introspection, and taking effective action are the practices that combine to create what I am calling your change intelligence factor. The first critical change practice is your ability to exert personal discipline made possible because you know who you are at a core place. This deep-seated self-awareness allows you to respond to events rather than react to them. Nothing kills a relationship faster than a knee-jerk reaction done in the heat of the moment. Even when/if you apologize, the memory of what you did or said lingers. The second critical change practice is your ability to think through what is happening on multiple levels for ultimate clarity. What you are developing here is the hindsight-to-foresight continuum, that is, your ability to step back from the story you tell yourself about an event and consider other interpretations, which you can then use to guide your future actions. This leads to the third critical change practice: your ability to take the most effective action open to you at a given point in time, assess the feedback you receive in real time, and then act again. The arena of action includes your conversational competence, your ability to engage others, and your ability to lead and contribute—all of which can make or break a career.

Intimately linked, these practices develop your ability to make the behavior changes current events are showing you are necessary. And your ability to change, to dance under pressure with grace and dignity, is critical to your success, professionally and personally. Working together, these practices foster your continuing development into a high-performing, contributing member of any organization. The bottom line is to learn how to change authentically—to embody the new you that is emerging—enabling you to keep your internal and external relationships strong and reap the rewards of doing business successfully.

Change intelligence plays out in your personal life as well. The bottom line personally is a rich and rewarding life of loving family and friends. Quite simply put, your change intelligence factor enables you to become extra-ordinary.

Things do not change, we change.
—Henry David Thoreau

1

Change Fundamentals: The Marriage
of Emotions and Change

*The significant problems we face cannot be solved at the same level
of thinking we were at when we created them.*
—Albert Einstein

As the competition for business intensifies, more is being asked of you as an employee, a manager, and a leader. Let's face it; creating a successful organization today is hard work. What worked yesterday doesn't work today. Traditional structures are giving way to more collaborative formats. Throw in the unique personalities, wants, and needs of a multigenerational, multicultural workforce, and the challenges increase exponentially.

And although it may feel like it at times, change is not the enemy. How you cope with it, however, could be. Your ability to be fleet of foot, to embrace new systems and processes often without a lot of explanation, to be present in the moment with your customers and direct reports, to honor all of your relationships, and to plan for an unpredictable future all combine to determine the level of success you achieve. Your challenge is intensified because organizational downsizing has increased your responsibilities while constrained budgets have decreased your access to the training that would help you meet the new requirements. It falls on your shoulders to do what you need to do, to learn what you need to learn, to do your job.

Though this may seem obvious, it is critical that you embrace the understanding that you are the primary actor in your life, that your actions generate the results you achieve. Think about your current circumstances. Are the actions you are taking right now enabling or hindering your effectiveness? What do you need to stop doing? What do you need to start doing? What do you need to learn? What do you need to change?

And an even harder question flows from these:

What are you resisting when you resist changing?

On the surface, these are simple questions. Dig deeper. Your answers are the keys to open various opportunity doors. Not answering or ignoring your answers keep these doors locked. Harness your courage, unlock the doors, and walk through. Notice what is working for you. Notice where you have breakdowns— those Murphy's law disruptive events that pull you off your game, throwing you off balance and out of sync. Assess how long it takes you to recover, regroup, and refocus.

Change intelligence asks you to take the energy you have been expending on not accepting what is happening and instead focus it like a laser on accepting what is, to come to peace with what is happening, and then to embrace learning as the vehicle to generate new possibilities for yourself. As you learn more about the issues that affect your own performance, you can begin to see where you can change your actions and incorporate new skills in ways that make sense for you.

Figure 1.1 The Change Intelligence Factor Continuum

Your ability to change travels along a scale or continuum (Figure 1.1). On the low end, you exhibit a total refusal to change. When your career stagnates, when you accept that you are stuck and make the conscious decision that being stuck is no longer acceptable, you are ready to change. As you face your fears, become more self-aware, and reassess your true abilities, you open yourself to new possibilities that fuel your capacity to change. You seek out new learning and begin the journey. Initiating new strategies in a disciplined way moves you toward the higher end of the continuum, where change becomes embodied and is as natural to you as breathing.

The benefits of undertaking the change intelligence journey are clear and often immediate. The first benefit will be stronger relationships—critically important because relationships determine options. Stronger relationships in turn produce the second benefit: more opportunities to explore. In fact, for the first time, you may establish a new coherence in your life. As you make sustainable changes in your behaviors, you progress higher along change intelligence factor continuum, enhancing your personal and career success.

> *It is not the strongest of the species that survives, nor the most intelligent, but the one most responsive to change.*
> *—Charles Darwin*

Change can be described as the point where something old stops and something new begins. Many books and studies focus on short-term gains made through change initiatives. While they supply reference models and delineate the change process steps to follow, the long-term success of many initiatives often proves elusive. Missing from most change models is what happens within you—those thoughts and feelings (fear, uneasiness, discomfort) that surface when any change is announced or when you recognize that what you are doing is no longer working and that you need to change. Sure, you can stifle these emotions, but often at costs ranging from poor buy-in and incomplete implementation to backsliding into old habits and outright obstruction or sabotage. The emotional component of any change must be acknowledged and addressed.

Figure 1.2 The Dynamic Change Model

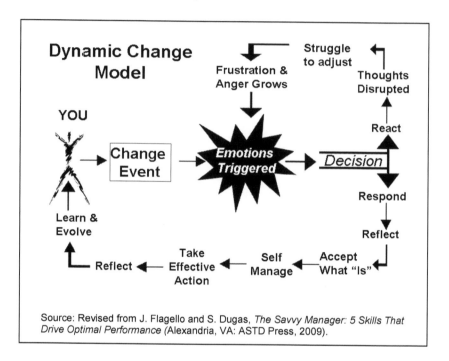

Source: Revised from J. Flagello and S. Dugas, *The Savvy Manager: 5 Skills That Drive Optimal Performance* (Alexandria, VA: ASTD Press, 2009).

The Dynamic Change Model (Figure 1.2) shows the process you undergo when you experience a change event. How you respond to the emotions triggered by a change event directly influences the actions you take. It is an iterative process, a continuous loop of you in action. The purpose of the model is to focus your attention on what is happening to you internally during any change event. You always have an action choice, which falls into one of two broad categories: reacting or responding.

Reacting is getting caught up in the emotion of an event and behaving in ways that may feel good in the moment but may prove detrimental long term. Your impulse control is replaced by the immediate condition that charges your actions. You are out of control, fueled by external events that compromise your effectiveness.

Unlike reacting, which is reflexive, *responding* is all about thoughtful choice. Responding is the highest form of personal freedom. What you are saying with and through your actions is that you are in charge of your own life. No excuses. Responding is value based, which is why self-awareness is the critical first practice of change intelligence. You have to know what you value, what you believe, and where you draw your lines in the sand. And responding is very powerful. You are choosing how you will act. The seeds that blossom from your choices become your life.

Notice in the model how the action decision point, the fork in the road, comes after you pass through an emotional field. Emotions have the potential to play a powerful role during change events. If you perceive the change to be minor or positive, choosing to respond is easy. You can adjust your performance and incorporate the new actions without much angst. Strong, negative emotions, however, cause you to react. Reacting further ignites powerful emotions. Anger, frustration, struggling to adjust, and resentment fuel one another and can lead you to get stuck in a destructive emotional loop—cycling through the stages shown in the upper right of the Dynamic Change Model, all the time thinking that the energy you are expending is solving the problem when it is only dragging you deeper into a downward spiral of negativity.

This is where change intelligence comes into play. Your decision about which path to take is a direct result of how you process your feelings about the event. As you develop your change intelligence you will find yourself making the response choice at the critical decision juncture. When you choose to respond, you move along the lower loop of the model. You reflect on what is happening and accept it. Then you discipline your actions to support what you believe responding means in the situation. Reflecting shows up again as you revisit the event and learn what you need to learn to grow.

If you find yourself in the reactive loop, caught up in an emotion-controlled downward spiral, change intelligence allows you to see your situation faster (reflecting on and accepting) and apply your internal brakes (self-discipline). At the critical decision point, when you could go either way, change intelligence helps you better assess what is happening and choose an appropriate response. You accept what is and let go of the need to like it. Acceptance brings calm and gives you more personal control. The emotions that emerge now might include curiosity, interest, patience, hope, and courage. You work through your options, seeking those that empower your actions to produce the results you really want without the baggage of fear, anger, or frustration. And you learn the lessons this experience is designed to teach you, tucking them away for the next time a change event does not immediately suit you.

> *Habit is the hell to which people cling*
> *in an attempt to stop the flow of change.*
> —*Carolyn Myss*

Developing Change Intelligence

Your current habits, behaviors, and attitudes are entrenched and often invisible until something triggers you to notice what you are doing. Think for a moment about the little things that you habitually do and say. Do you grit your teeth, twirl your hair, tap your pencil, constantly check your cell phone, doodle during meetings? Do you have phrases that infuse your speech or that you blurt out without thinking like "you've got to be kidding" "you know" or "I don't care." The purpose of these questions is to get you to become aware of simple habits. Now make a conscious effort to stop doing one, just one. Breaking the grip of habit requires mindfulness and commitment. It takes considerable effort to first notice what you are doing, then initiate new behaviors, and finally reinforce their repetitive use. These are all part and parcel of growing your change intelligence factor. In most cases, changing proves easy to say and hard to do.

You may not even notice that the behaviors that support your effectiveness in the short term are sabotaging your personal development in the long term. Consider Ann who wanted a promotion to division director at a consumer products company when her manager retired at the end of the quarter. She knew she needed to delegate more and prepare Ben, a competent employee, to replace her. She also knew she needed to surpass her normal production goals. To achieve both goals, Ann spent hours with Ben reviewing his plans, overseeing his every decision to make certain no mistakes would undermine his potential promotion or the department's results upon which her own promotion depended. A new production process idea Ben suggested had potential but was not the way Ann liked things done. Ben sensed he did not have her full support and abandoned his idea so that he would not jeopardize his promotion opportunity. Unfortunately, Ann did not get the promotion because she was seen as indispensable in her current position, and management felt Ben was too tentative and needed more time to grow.

In this example, Ann's competing needs surfaced. Her need to have things done her way interfered with her need to delegate more and groom a possible replacement. Competing needs are common; their emotional pull strong. Even as you may sincerely want something different, you also want the comfort and security of what is familiar.

Even when you have your emotional act together and choose responding (that is, taking the lower right path on the Dynamic Change Model), events have their own way of unfolding. Things will happen that further challenge your resolve and make you question your decisions. An unexpected outcome, a thoughtless action by a co-worker, or a snarly retort can easily pull you right back into the downward spiral of reacting. It is important to stay vigilant and work through issues as they surface in ways that support your opportunities.

Here is another example. A new process is introduced at work that changes your daily routine. You go along to get along, but the voice in your head is having a "heated hissy fit." Whether you realize it or not, you are reacting to events around you. You may find it hard to fully concentrate and perform the new process. You feel edgy and anxious as fiery emotions drain your energy. You complain outwardly, or just between your own ears, that the new system is taking longer. You are frustrated by the newness and miss the familiar old routine. You are spiraling deeper and deeper through the Dynamic Change Model's reactive cycle.

Change intelligence strengthens your ability to recognize and stop your downward spiral more quickly. As you again reach the decision point, you consciously seek out different actions. You are "sick and tired of being sick and tired." You begin to think about what it would take to respond differently—what it would look like, what it would feel like. You shift to a new approach, beginning with accepting what is happening. You discipline your actions to make the required changes that both reduce your stress and align your thoughts and emotions. You consciously decide what outcome you want, which empowers your actions. You realize that as you shift your internal perceptions and outward actions, things actually appear to get better. Your internal stress level diminishes and you struggle less. You get yourself back in balance, ready for the next changes that are sure to follow.

Through new learning you can expand your repertoire of response possibilities. You become generative and can adapt to increasing complexity with transformative insight. As you learn how to discipline your own behaviors and actions in ways that benefit you and your organization, your effectiveness as a knowledge worker, manager, and leader grows. Your position on the change intelligence factor continuum moves a notch or two toward mastery.

> *By my actions . . . teach my mind.*
> *—William Shakespeare*

Insights for Action

Every situation exists in an emotional field. Your decisions and actions intensify the emotional field, stabilize it, or minimize it. For some situations, the decision process is a snap. For other situations, making a decision is a long and thoughtful process. Not deciding constitutes a decision regardless of whether putting off making a decision is a stalling tactic to work through the ramifications of your actions, or you are too fearful of possible results to act. You want to avoid knee-jerk reactions during the flashpoint of anger that you may regret for a lifetime. The choice is yours.

Your true power blossoms as your change intelligence grows. Change is first and foremost a heart act. Then it becomes a head act. You can temper emotions with more rational thought only after you experience and acknowledge them. Stifling that experiential element denies you the benefit of important learning. Cultivating the signals all of your senses are sending you gives you the gift of response and is a surefire way to more fully harness emotion's power in support of desired outcomes.

> *Not everything that is faced can be changed,*
> *but nothing can be changed until it is faced.*
> *—James Baldwin*

ACTIVITY: Experiment with Change

Do one thing differently today. Take a different route to work. Bring your lunch if you always go out. Go out for an hour if you usually eat at your desk. Send out the agenda for tomorrow's meeting. It does not have to be a big change. Notice what happens when you change something simple.

- What was the impact on your performance?

- How did you impact the performance of others?

- What emotions, if any, were triggered?

- Did your day become easier or more difficult?

- Were your results more to your liking?

ACTIVITY: Talk about Change

At your next department meeting, initiate a change discussion. Select one event to be the focus for the discussion. It can be about a change that is currently being implemented or a new change that you would like to see implemented. Ask everyone to answer the following questions.

Considering change event "x":

As a department:
- What are we doing that supports this new initiative and helps promote its success?

- What actions are we taking that minimize or hinder the success of this initiative?

- What can our department do differently that would prove more helpful.

As an individual member of this team:
- What can I do as a member of this team to better ensure the success of this initiative?

- What do I need to stop doing?

2

Practices to Grow Your
Change Intelligence

*We invest so much in what we know
that we refuse to give it up,
even when it has stopped serving us.*
—Julio Olalla

You may be thinking that something needs to change—and fast. You're stressed, frustrated that things are taking longer than you anticipated they would. You look around and see people and processes that drive you crazy, that don't seem fair, that appear out of control. You wish the proverbial "they" would start doing this, or stop doing that. But you can't change other people. You can only change you. So where do you start?

The most important element of any change effort is what is going on inside you. To change anything "out" there, you must first get a grip on what is going on "in" here. The starting point is always you. Your life is the culmination of your experiences to date and the stories you have developed around those experiences. Whether you cast yourself as hero or victim, your stories frame your relationships, which in turn create your outcomes and your life. The baggage you carry—every assessment you make about yourself, others, and events—determines the moves open to you.

Your change intelligence—the capacity to see change as beneficial and boldly embrace the opportunities it presents—is rooted in how you process events. You construct the situations you experience by virtue of how you relate to them. Furthermore, you can change how you show up. Even the smallest change you adopt can have enormous positive ramifications on your relationships, your career, and those you serve. Utilizing the power of change intelligence effectively opens your connective systems and your neural networks to new learning, expanding your options. The good news is that you can strengthen your internal operating system, empowering you to engage at your highest level of performance in what is clearly a very complex world.

To help frame this discussion, think about the people you admire:

- What words describe the qualities you admire in them?

- What about these people makes you want to have a relationship with them?

- What actions do they take that show others that they care?

Now think about the behaviors and skill set that you use every day. Do you see any of the traits you admire in others in your own actions? It takes courage to consciously peel back your internal layers of self so you can truly see what you do and how you do it. The crucial question to consider is how well your behaviors and skills are working for you now. When you undertake this type of exploration, you begin to see behaviors you are proud of—as well as those that may be embarrassing. You notice where there might be gaps in your performance that diminish your effectiveness.

Today's workplace asks more of you than ever before. To succeed you must come prepared to be an active contributor to the solution and not be seen as part of the problem. Three critical change practices work together to build your capacity to ground your actions, make sustainable personal changes, and create the outcomes you truly want: self-discipline through self-awareness, introspection, and taking effective actions. As you read the description of each practice in Figure 2.1, make a hash mark on the continuum to represent your current assessment of how well you incorporate each behavior into your daily actions. Then think about what it would take—what actions would you need to change—to move you closer to a higher degree of effectiveness.

Figure 2.1 Three Practices to Build Change Intelligence

Practice 1: Develop Discipline through Awareness: Know Yourself —Control Yourself
You must understand your own drives and motivations so you can discipline your actions and leverage your effectiveness to produce the results you really want.

Unaware &		Aware &
Out of Control		In Full Control
(low)		(high)

Practice 2: Expand Your Perceptions: Embrace the Gift of Introspection
You must be able to think things through, see the subtle nuances of events, and observe how your own perceptions and meaning-making system color your thinking and influence your ability to deliver successful outcomes.

| Internally Blind | | Keenly Insightful |
| (low) | | (high) |

Practice 3: Take Effective Actions: Apply Focus and Choice
You must constantly refine your own behaviors based on your growing insights to ensure that the actions you take produce the results you really want.

| Knee-jerk Reactions | | Refined Responses |
| (low) | | (high) |

As you incorporate each practice into your action repertoire, you will begin to feel more comfortable with change. You will notice a new confidence growing inside you. Your conversation capabilities are enhanced because you are able to say what you mean in ways that others can hear and appreciate as honest and real. You are more able to engage in meaningful relationships and you can resolve conflicts more effectively. Your influence grows because you strive to empower rather than control others. At ease in your own skin, you mature into a more authentic version of yourself: a stronger individual actor, a source of inspiration for others to emulate, a supportive partner, and an effective contributor to the larger organization.

The kind of life you live tomorrow begins in your mind today.
—Joe Batten

Practice 1: Develop Discipline through Awareness: Know Yourself–Control Yourself

Knowing others is intelligence; knowing yourself is true wisdom.
Mastering others is strength; mastering yourself is true power.
—Tao Te Ching

Consider this critically important question: If you do not know who you are, how can you ever hope to develop the types of honest relationships that fully empower you to become your best? Other questions quickly emerge about your ability to act with authenticity, connect with others, and build vibrant, trustworthy relationships that are the cornerstones of a great life. What new learning or new awareness about who you are and who you want to become will best support your efforts and align with your goals?

From a business perspective, if you cannot manage yourself, how can you ever hope to manage others? What does it mean to discipline your actions and manage yourself? What skills will you need to learn in order to discipline and control your own actions? How can you generate effective personal discipline mechanisms to foster collaborative efforts with others, both personally and professionally? How will you model excellent performance? How will you be able to influence and truly lead? What needs to change about you?

Knowing yourself is the process through which you increase your awareness of your underlying motivations in order to more effectively direct and control your performance and your results. This relationship is clearly shown in the continuum for practice 1 that follows:

You must understand your own drives and motivations, so you can discipline your actions and leverage your effectiveness to produce the results you really want.

Unaware ⟵——————————⟶ Aware
Out of   In Full
Control   Control
(low)   *(high)*

The benefits of self-knowledge are clear. When you drill down and clarify what truly motivates you and set your boundaries, you will find it easier to discipline your actions to achieve your goals. This walk toward awareness will also make you acutely aware of those behaviors and actions that diminish your effectiveness. Choosing to stop actions that undermine your success is an empowering component of self-discipline. As your awareness of your underlying motivations grows, your increasing change intelligence will help you explore new ways to take more disciplined, powerful, and effective actions on your own behalf.

L-E-B Model (Language, Emotion, Body)

There are many models that seek to help people understand the contexts or domains within which human beings experience life. One very useful model, the L-E-B Model, designed by the Newfield Network, Inc., helps to visually express the three primary learning domains that guide actions. From a holistic perspective, the L-E-B

Model offers you a way to sharpen your learning abilities and make conscious personal changes that align with your goals (Figure 2.2).

Figure 2.2 The L-E-B Model

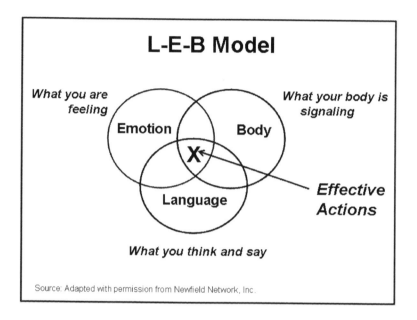

Source: Adapted with permission from Newfield Network, Inc.

In this model, *L* is the language or mental/cognitive domain. Most people consider language to be their primary learning domain. Language is the code used to express thoughts and frame interpretations. Through language you make distinctions and establish the context within which you live your life. In many ways, language actually creates your world. With a simple "yes" or "no," you open and close opportunities.

E is the emotional domain. Included here is the mood within which you embrace life as well as situations where an event triggers an immediate emotional outburst. One person may live in a mood of optimism, believing that anything is possible. Certain actions are available to this kind of person while others are not. Another person may live in a mood of resentment or despair, blaming others for his or her lot in life and unwilling to initiate new actions to change the results he or she is getting. There are many other possible mood fields, such as sadness, ambition, joy, confidence, pessimism, and peace. Often people swing between different moods depending on circumstances. I'll explore moods and emotions in more detail later in this chapter. For now, just take a moment to think about your own emotional field and the kind of life it is creating for you.

B is the body or somatic domain, your kinesthetic intelligence. Often cited as the unused intelligence, the body is an untapped wealth of information. Most people need to learn how to pay attention to what their bodies are trying to tell them. Think about how stress shows up in your body. Does your breathing become shallow? Do your shoulders tighten? Do you get a headache? What happens in your body when you have to depend on someone else or when others are depending on you? Becoming more attuned to the messages your body is sending you is one sure way to expand your self-awareness.

The *X* in the middle represents the space where you are most effective; where what you are thinking/saying, feeling (emotionally), and sensing (physically) are all in synchronistic harmony. The more aligned these learning domains are, the larger this area of intersection becomes, which expands your ability to take effective actions. Simply stated, you give your best performance when what you think, say, and feel (emotionally and physically) are working together.

How you expand or diminish these three domains is unique to you. You might squash or totally ignore one domain and enlarge another. You may be thinking that language plays the more pronounced role in your learning and thus your life. After all, reading, writing, thinking, and speaking are all actions rooted in language. However, if you think about a time when you were ill or your emotions were charged, you can begin to see the impact the domains of body and emotions have on you. Both could easily undermine anything you may be attempting through the language domain.

To better understand how your learning domains support your effectiveness, think of the interconnecting circles shown in Figure 2.2 as the three rings magicians often use in their acts. Like the magician's rings, these domains overlap. They flex and move with and against one another, opening and closing your action possibilities. For example, think of the times you said "yes," but the voice inside your head was screaming "no." Could you feel your body tighten as your words did not match your feelings? What did this disconnect between what you said and what you were thinking do to your stress level? When you did what you didn't want to do, what were the results? Could they have been better had you wanted to do it? What would it have taken mentally, emotionally, and physically to garner the courage to say "no" and offer an alternative way to get the task done?

Let's use the L-E-B Model to solidify the concept. Consider this simple scenario. One of your team members tells you he's put in a vacation time request for the three days before Thanksgiving, sharing his plans for the annual deer hunting trip with friends. His absence will definitely add to your workload. Your inner voice screams the dialogue below, triggered by your own feelings of being overworked:

> Deer hunting! Is he for real? I can't remember when I had time to go hunting, let alone do anything else I want to do. Who does this guy think he is? Can't he see we are short-handed? How can he ask to take off to go hunting?

What you do next could make or break your relationship with this person, your reputation in the department, or even your career. Figure 2.3 diagrams this internal dialogue. Assume a starting place with your domains of action centered and in balance. There are three action possibilities offered for your consideration.

Figure 2.3 The L-E-B Model in Action

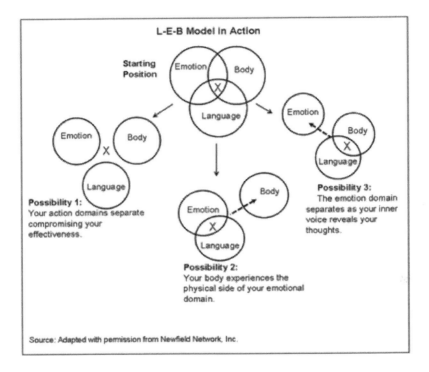

The language domain (possibility 1) is the easiest to notice and once compromised can derail your power and damage your relationship. Your tone, volume, and word choice could be affected as your inner voice builds the case against this guy and the unfairness of it all. Reacting too fast could cause you to say things in the heat of the moment; words that cannot easily (or perhaps ever) be erased or forgotten.

The body domain works much the same way as your emotions, moving in and out as you physically react or respond to what is occurring. In possibility 2, you might experience a clenched jaw, popping veins in your neck, or an increase in blood pressure. You might unconsciously move your body into a more aggressive position, with legs braced and arms crossed. These are body expressions triggered by your emotions, and they all cause your body domain to disconnect.

Possibility 3 shows the *E* circle disconnecting from the other two. Here, the emotions take charge. This is not your finest emotionally intelligent hour. In terms of the Dynamic Change Model from chapter 1, your inner dialogue is clearly reacting to the hunting trip news. In most instances the emotions you experience about an event will arise before the language you use to describe it.

What do you do next? The point to realize here is that you have options. Although there is no one right action to take, your effectiveness grows when your language, emotion, and body domains come together, not when they separate. Consider possibility 3 taking the lead in the deer hunting trip example. Unless and until you recognize that your emotions are driving the situation, any actions you take (in word or deed) could jeopardize your relationship with this person. And solid relationships are vital to your ability to influence and achieve long-term success.

There are several strategies that you can use to regain self-control before you act:

- *Take a breath*. Take a few deep breaths to reduce the impact of the emotional trigger this trip announcement created for you. As you slowly inhale and exhale you allow the physical manifestation of your emotions to pass through you.

- *Take a moment.* Give yourself time to consider the longer term implications of your next actions and make the all-important brain-to-mouth connection.

- ***Choose and time your words carefully.*** You may want to express a point of view about your increased workload and how this request makes you feel, but the smarter strategy is to look for ways to hold a more powerful conversation at a crucial juncture, one that will maintain the relationship with your colleague and solve the more immediate workload increase problem.

This example clearly shows the critically important role that personal discipline (practice 1) plays in change intelligence.

It is not enough to have great qualities.
We should also have the management of them.
—La Rochefoucauld

Manage Your Meaning-Making System

Although we will explore your meaning-making system more completely under practice 2, at this point I want you to begin to notice the meaning you are attaching to your experiences and the power of this often-invisible force. All of us attach meaning to the events that happen to us. It is the only way we can function. Meaning is the story we create, the narrative that frames what happens to us, and it drives action. Your inner assessor is the voice that judges your thoughts and creates the distinctions that manifest as the actions you take, those you don't take, and those that aren't even on your radar screen, and therefore, you never consider. Sometimes your inner voice takes poetic license, embellishing past events, giving them more meaning and importance than they might deserve in the current context. Would a different interpretation of past events serve you better? How might an alternative view prove more fruitful to you in the present time?

Learning to recognize the internal conversation that is directing your actions is vital to your success. If it helps, picture two characters, one perched on each shoulder. One is whispering self-limiting dialogue in one ear, while the other is murmuring confidence-building words into the other ear. Who are you listening to? What is still true about you? What is no longer relevant? Remember Henry Ford's famous quote: "Whether you think you can or think you can't, you're right."

The important learning here is the explicit recognition that you have your thoughts; not that whatever you are thinking or feeling has hooked you. You have an internal system that ascribes meaning to your experiences and thoughts and that system can be changed if it isn't serving your best interests. When you can challenge the current contextual validity of your meaning-making system, your change intelligence grows because you are able to choose more appropriate responses. Perhaps you see that old behaviors, which might have served you in the past, are now detrimental to your performance. You might finally realize that you are not the shy person you were in high school, that you have grown and are able to make significant contributions. You might uncover what is at the heart of your fears as a first step toward overcoming them. Or reveal your blind spots and character flaws so that you can begin to work on them. As you become aware of your own humanness, you can more easily appreciate and value the humanness of others.

When you learn how to grow from the inside out, to be internally centered, you can become self-generating. Your autopilot switch is off. Forgoing external approval or validation, you monitor and own your actions. You are in charge of yourself: what you say, what you think, how you feel, and how all of that gets outwardly expressed. You are fully present in the moments of your life, focused on what you can do now to move closer to your goals. Exerting discipline over your actions connects you to what is important in your life. Even when you falter, the inner strength now growing inside you reminds you of your capacity to learn. With practice, what appears to be a long process will happen in a heartbeat.

Knowing is not enough; we must apply.
Willing is not enough; we must do.
—Goethe

Develop Emotional Discipline

Learning how to control your emotional energy is crucial to growing your change intelligence capabilities. Although both are housed within the *E* domain circle, there are actually two energies at play: emotion energy and mood energy. Emotions are strong feelings that are triggered by some event or situation. Emotion energy is always present in some form, usually experienced as subjective responses to both pleasant and unpleasant experiences. For example, you feel overjoyed that your team had the best sales figures for the quarter. You get an unexpected email from an old college friend and find yourself tearful, remembering the fun you once shared. Or, you may become frustrated when you witness a colleague giving poor quality service to an important client and are conflicted since you know that intervening will make an already bad situation worse. Triggered emotions show up in your body first, before they become words and actions. As shown in the Dynamic Change Model in chapter 1 (Figure 1.1), when an event activates an emotion, you can react or respond. You might walk away giving yourself time to cool down, you could completely shut down and close yourself off from others, or you could be abrupt or even throw an adult temper tantrum. Each pattern has its own consequences, both good and bad. Which seems to fit you and when?

Mood energy differs from emotion energy in that aside from any specific event, you live your life in a certain mood; your way of being, how you tune yourself into the world, how you naturally show up. Mood transparently informs how you engage and ground your relationships with others. Your mood at work can be different than your mood at home with family and friends. Your mood is not hard-wired into your being. As you become more self-aware, you gain more control over how you present yourself. Past assessments that may be fueling a certain mood can be challenged in ways that allow you to shift your mood and open new possibilities. Change intelligence's strongest benefit is that it enables you to embrace moods that better serve you.

Take the mood of resignation prevalent in many workplaces today. It lives in your effort-to-outcome assessment. When you assess that nothing you do can change your future at work, you live in a mood of resignation. You see yourself stuck in your job, and since you believe nothing you do will change that, you don't bother doing anything. If you were to garner your courage, dust off your resume, and apply for a new position with a different company and get the job, that experience, predicated on you changing your behavior (applying for the job), would challenge your previous assessment that nothing you did mattered. Resignation's hold over you would decrease ever so slightly because you changed what you did and got a different result. You constructed a different future for yourself by virtue of one small action. What else could your actions change? Both emotions and moods are energies that position you to take, or prevent you from taking, certain actions based on what you are thinking and how you are feeling.

> *The measure of intelligence is the ability to change.*
> *—Albert Einstein*

Insights for Action

Practice 1 is all about you. Becoming more self-aware places you in the driver's seat of your life. You can make conscious choices. And self-awareness is the lever to discipline your actions. The benefit is clear. Strong self-knowledge and self-discipline skills build confidence, growing your capacity to face challenges and fears head on. You develop awareness that takes you to higher levels of performance beyond what you need for your job. Especially in uncertain times, personal control and resiliency are required to adapt to changing circumstances. Self-managing skills allow you to be clear about your motives and uncover your blind spots. You recognize when you are "talking trash" or when your ego inflates your sense of self-importance.

Expanding the discussion to managerial responsibilities, current workplace demands require heightened consciousness about how your efforts and those of your co-workers contribute to the larger organizational goals. As you become more self-generating (producing what you need from within yourself) and self-correcting (making changes as needed), your performance improves. Fears diminish and you are able to engage in higher level conversations with others, thereby enhancing the results collaboratively produced. Knowing and controlling yourself allows your authenticity to shine through and elicits the trust that most organizations claim to want and are at a loss to create.

CASE STUDY

Here is a story about Sue who had some growing up to do. Just when she was to ascend to the position of the plant manager, her own history with the very people she would need to support her in her new position appeared problematic. After reading the case, answer the questions based on what you believe you would do assist Sue.

Sue was eager to become the first female plant manager at the paper mill. Her participation in the company's management training program right out of college had paid off, earning her promotion after promotion in a man's world. She was smart and confident, strongly advocating for her own ideas at meetings, which often rubbed her colleagues the wrong way. When her less-than-collaborative style was brought to her attention by her manager, Sue feigned regret and promised to mend her ways. Within a short time, her next great idea hit pay dirt for the company, gave her another ego boost, and all was forgiven. Her staff was supportive of her goal to become plant manager because they saw their promotions and success tied to hers. In

Sue's mind, she had to be tougher, stronger, and more aggressive than her male counterparts. She ignored any perceived resentment from her peers, which usually showed up as them staying in the background, letting her take the lead while silently praying that this time she would fail. Sue was quickly becoming the epitome of a one-woman show, staking her reputation on being the best at what she did, leaving others to eat her dust.

Now that her promotion was safely in hand, Sue was basking in the accolades of senior management's approval as they shepherded her visits to various plants and introduced her at the stockholders annual meeting. In the quiet moments of her nights alone in strange hotels, however, a sense of dread was beginning to surface. The people she would need the most seemed to be keeping their distance. In the recesses of her mind she knew that she could not really run the mill alone without their help and full support. How to enlist that support was robbing her sleep and invading her dreams.

- What questions might you ask Sue to help her see the impact of her past actions with her staff more clearly?

- What actions would you coach Sue to embrace to rebuild her relationships?

- What new personal disciplines does Sue need to embrace?

- How might you coach Sue as she reconstitutes her sense of self in her new role?

- What language, emotion, and body distinctions will best help Sue?

ACTIVITY: Directing Emotional Energies

Consider these common workplace situations. What would your most likely action be?

- You are at a meeting with company leaders and someone challenges you about your findings.

- A less experienced person just got the promotion you were hoping for and believed you had earned.

- Your print order is not ready at the time promised.

- A co-worker tells you your opinion is wrong at a meeting in front of your boss and peers.

- One of your direct reports just did what you specifically told him/her not to do.

- You receive several emails praising your recent sales presentation.

- You just found out that you are the only manager to receive a bonus.

Analyze Your Findings

- Which behaviors strengthen your position and reputation?

- Which reactions diminish your personal power?

- Which emotions make you appear weak and do not bring out your best?

- Which triggers seem to carry over into other areas of your life?

- What change can you begin to make that will direct your emotional energies in ways that better serve you?

- How does your new learning about personal discipline and the L-E-B Model facilitate more effective actions on your part?

Identify two specific behaviors that will foster your emotional intelligence growth. What is your plan to incorporate each one into your daily actions?

Practice 2: Expand Your Perceptions: Embrace the Gift of Introspection

> *The range of what we think and do is*
> *limited by what we fail to notice.*
> *And because we fail to notice that we*
> *fail to notice, there is little we can do*
> *to change, until we notice how failing*
> *to notice shapes our thoughts and deeds.*
> —R. D. Laing

The proverbial riddle about which came first, the chicken or the egg, aptly starts the discussion about the relationship between thinking and acting. Does thinking things through help you discipline your actions better? Or must you act first (by exerting self-discipline) to make the space to be able to step back, observe what is happening, and see the bigger picture, which then allows you to take more effective actions? In practice, it is impossible to develop one capability without also developing the other.

Appreciating how you see your world is a crucial starting point for exerting change intelligence. Introspection's gift is that it introduces you to that part of yourself that is the observer—the part that informs your meaning-making system and powers your actions. Building your observer skills forces you to become more self-aware, which in turn strengthens your ability to discipline your actions because you can more clearly define your priorities. Your capacity for introspection, practice 2, falls on a continuum ranging from internal blindness to keenly insightful.

You must be able to think things through, see the subtle nuances of events, observe how your own perceptions and meaning-making system color your thinking and influence your ability to deliver successful outcomes.

Internally Blind ←————————→ Keenly Insightful
(low)   *(high)*

As you intentionally employ deeper-level reflective strategies, you can examine your mental, emotional, and physical domains, breaking the transparency of your actions and consciously drawing out a more complete, nonjudgmental, and insightful image of yourself. You illuminate unspoken motivations or competing needs at work and in your personal life. You expose the subtle nuances, constructed meanings, automatic assessments, assumptions, and interpretations that frame your actions, holding them up for scrutiny and examination.

Through introspection you begin to connect the dots between what you claim to want, your interpretation about what is happening around you, the actions you are taking, and the results you are getting. You stop complaining outwardly because you accept that you are the only person who can initiate actions to change your situation. You contemplate the gap, what's missing, and assess the processes and techniques you are using to close the gap. Then you probe deeper, do some soul searching, and figure out what is really missing. Most often, what is really missing is linked to an internal assessment you are making about your own abilities. Because your interpretations lead to your actions, your ability to ground your meaning-making system in a current context is important. Isolating the variables that you are using to make the case for or against a certain action or point of view surface. As insights about what "is" are accepted, new possibilities emerge. Your change intelligence capitalizes on your new insights allowing you to actually do something different—change.

> *The true journey of discovery does not consist of searching*
> *for new territories but in having new eyes.*
> *—Marcel Proust*

Explore Your Observer

Did you ever walk out of a staff meeting with a colleague who was very upset about something that was said but you perceived as no big deal? You scratched your head, confused about why your colleague was "going off the deep end." You may have wondered what he saw that you didn't see; what he heard that you didn't hear. If you were to compare your descriptions of what transpired during the meeting, you may be surprised to find you each have unique versions of the same incident.

What is really happening here is the intersection of different observers. You are a certain type of observer. Your spouse, manager, team members, or friends are all different types of observers. Each of you sees the world through your own created filters. To make matters worse, most people are blind to their filters. Some people even believe that their way of seeing is the only way.

Often invisible, the observer that you are cannot change or act anew on what it cannot see. The question to ask is whether your perceptual filters support the outcomes you want or work against you? Are you the victim (glass half empty) or the victor (glass half full)? Think about it. If your observer filters through the lens of "he who dies with the most toys wins," how does that color your interpretations and lead you to take certain actions? If your observer filters through the lens of "there is more than enough for all of us," what actions would that filter encourage?

In the end, the actions you take support the status quo of your filtered world view. And more important, what you observe is inextricably linked to you, the person who is doing the observing. Observing is not an objective action. Have an artist share what she sees when she looks at the *Mona Lisa*. Compare her description with what you see. You will become acutely aware of how different people with different experiences and reference frames see the same things differently. Observing is highly subjective and directly linked to your current state of mind, emotions, physical well-being, and experiences. The need then is to make the invisible visible.

Let's examine how most people operate (Figure 2.4). The model on the left of the figure shows the traditional process. You act, you get a result, you act again. This is the standard operating process most people use, and for routine tasks it works well. It falls short, however, when you want to produce results that are different from those you usually get or during more complex or unprecedented events.

Figure 2.4 Action Processing Models

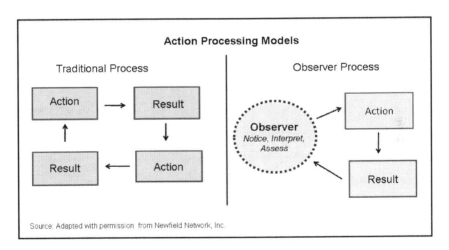

The model on the right of the figure adds the observer position. It is here that you step out of the automatic cause–effect / action–result cycle and contemplate the totality of what is happening. It is here that you work to expose your filters. And it is here that your change intelligence can begin to have an impact. You pause, step back, and learn how to "see" yourself in action and how you frame events. Within the pause, you invite other possible perspectives into the mix. Think of it as an out-of-body experience in real time.

You are actually doing three things when you draw on your observer: nonjudgmental noticing, interpreting, and assessing (Figure 2.5).

Figure 2.5 Your Observer in Action

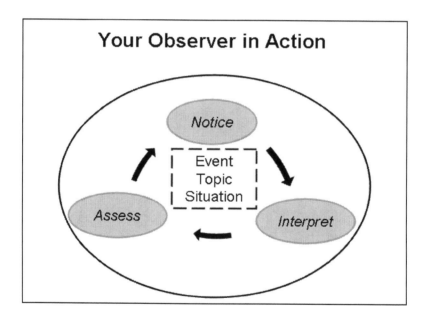

Noticing. To start, settle into a comfortable chair, take a few deep breaths, and work to clear your mind. Begin to focus on your subject, bringing it to mind. At this point, your only task is to notice, to bear witness to what is unfolding before you without judgment.

As you focus on a particular relationship, problem, topic, or issue of concern, notice how your mind is ordering the details. Become aware of any bias or filters your observer might be using.

Interpreting. This is where the story about events and relationships gets created. Keep in mind that any explanation is an interpretation, one among many possible interpretations. It is neither fact nor truth. Seriously examine how you are assigning meaning to the interactions to weave the story you are holding. What emotions are showing up? Is your story covering up actions that may not put you in the best light? Because meaning triggers behaviors, it opens and closes possibilities for you. You can gain a clearer picture of your own interpretive framework and the filters through which you assign meaning. You may also discover real areas where you have some inner work to do—where you need to expand your self-awareness, explore your self-concept, and exert more discipline and control going forward.

It is beneficial at this point to develop competing interpretations of the same events. For example, if you are the marketing person arguing for money to be allocated to a new campaign, what might the accounting person think of the proposed expenses? What energies are triggered as you consider these? As your picture grows, work to see the nuances of the situation. You might hypothesize different interpretations of the occurrence and consider motives behind actions. Notice the emergence of any conflicts or hidden agendas. How does shifting your observer to a different point of view make your interpretations and understanding richer?

Assessing. The final observer task is to make impact assessments. If you are reflecting on an important relationship, you could assess whether or not your current actions are moving the relationship in the direction you want it to go. If you are assessing an event like the morning's pre-launch meeting for a new product marketing campaign, you might assess whether your actions during the meeting enhanced or diminished your possibilities. Did your actions emanate from a sense of fear or possible loss? Did you act with honor and dignity or is shame or guilt cropping up? You can expand your assessments to your team, company, and other stakeholders. If you were in their shoes, how might the event enhance or diminish their possibilities? The infamous "win-win" label is really an assessment made about how to proceed after considering the ramifications of an event.

The past has a vote, but not a veto.
—Mordecai Kaplan

Two scenarios can help you fully understand the impact of your observer on your actions. Imagine that you are on your way to deliver the keynote address at the annual sales meeting. Your mind is on the presentation you plan to deliver. Blaring horns! Brakes! The taxi you are riding in has just had a close encounter with another car. While only a fender bender, there are two screaming drivers in the middle of the road. You have someplace important to be and neither of these people cares. All three of you are standing in different spaces, with different needs and concerns, and wanting different results.

Now consider the same scenario with a different flash point. You are still on your way to deliver a keynote address, but your phone rings and it is your boss telling you that you just landed the big account you were working on. Picture the circles of the L-E-B model (Figure 2.2) in your mind and ask yourself the following questions for each scenario:

- How are you feeling right now?

- How's your breathing?

- What else might you be experiencing physically?

- What thoughts are racing through your head?

- What do you need to do now to ensure that either scenario will not adversely affect your speech's delivery?

Your observer at any given point in time takes cues from the intersection of your personal L-E-B Model in real time. Mood and emotional state play important roles. In both scenarios your *E* circle is probably disconnected and you may find yourself on an emotional roller coaster. You could be so excited about winning the new account that your energy overtakes your message and your speech is too forceful, delivered too fast for the audience to grasp its full effect. The accident might have caused you to arrive just as you are called to the stage. It might force you to rush, and the increased adrenalin could make you appear nervous and jumpy on stage. You may be experiencing a minor case of whiplash that detracts from your concentration. A co-worker could mention a key piece of information about your topic before you go on stage which could further compromise your efforts. All of these experiences challenge your energy and require strong observer muscles be in place.

Strengthening your observer muscles allows you to broaden your possibilities because it invites new learning to inform your actions. It is the cornerstone to growing your change intelligence factor. Getting to this advanced level is the result of initiating a consistent introspective practice. Although it is far easier to just keep doing what you've been doing, the benefits of adding a reflective practice to your daily repertoire more than compensates for the effort. As you expose context and get to know the observer that lives inside you, new interpretations surface that generate a new awareness about who you are now and who you can become tomorrow.

As you build your observer skills, you are more able to consider the full spectrum of what you are doing to produce the results you are getting. You can examine the thought process and meaning-making systems that led you to this place at this time. You notice what felt right and what didn't. And you receive a gift—the gift of insight that ignites your change intelligence. You can change what you are doing, how you are doing it, and where you are doing it. And like many of the new processes discussed here, the more you activate your observer, the easier it becomes to shift into this space. In time, it becomes embodied as your natural operating system.

> *We see the world not as it is but as we are.*
> *—Albert Einstein*

Put Your Theories into Action

As you grow the observer that you are, another distinction may be revealed. You may notice a gap between two theories of action: the actions you talk about (espoused) versus the actions that you actually practice and use (Argyris and Schoen 1974). Your theories of action are based on your personal mental maps: your picture of reality. These pictures or maps unfold from your meaning-making system and sustain your perceptions and points of view, which in turn lead to your behaviors.

Meet Scott, a fulfillment center manager at a plastics plant. He embraced the popular open door management strategy. He believed that leaving his door open all the time sent a message of availability to his staff. After a difficult day, Scott went for a run to clear his mind and think about what was happening at the office. Two realizations crystallized for him. First, he realized how impatient he got when someone just came in and sat down in his office, especially when he is in the middle of something he assessed as important. Thinking back to that morning when Jim had stopped by to chat, he could still sense tension in his body even after several hours had passed. He remembered how he avoided making eye contact with Jim. And, he kept doing his work, hoping Jim would get the message that he was busy and leave. Worse yet, he remembered his responses were sharp and could have been construed as somewhat demeaning.

Scott's second "aha" realization centered on the recognition that there were times when his own projects required his full attention and concentration. These projects were equally as important to the company's success as were his staff interactions. The more he thought about it, the clearer it became that his open door was not working for everyone concerned. He began to consider alternatives that would allow him to finish his own work and still enhance his one-on-one staff interactions.

The simple act of taking time to clarify what's really happening and the results produced often reveals critical disconnects. When you expand your understanding of how you view and hold the world around you and the people within your world, a larger repertoire of behaviors and possibilities for action emerges. Becoming intimate with your observer is a simple idea really, and it may be just what is needed.

> *Only when the clamor of the outside world is silenced*
> *will you be able to hear the deeper vibration.*
> *Listen carefully.*
> *—Sarah Ban Breathnach*

Insights for Action

The underlying premise of change practice 2 is that you are an individual with a unique history and future. And as an employee, you are also part of the larger community of your company made up of people just like you, individuals with unique histories and desired futures. The goal is to network all of the energy of these unique people, so that the one becomes the powerful many. And introspection's gift holds tremendous promise as it enables you to think about how you are interacting with your colleagues. Your words and actions, your ability to listen, and your demeanor are all elements that either ignite creative outcomes or stifle excellence. The commitment to your colleagues must reflect your capacity to honor a strong connection to one another as equals.

Thinking more holistically, you are truly embracing the notion that the whole is more than a sum of its parts. If you are in a leadership role, you are charged with getting work done with and through others. You must ensure that the skills and capabilities of each employee contribute to desired results and that you hold an accurate appraisal of the members of your team. How can you inspire employees and gain their commitment to a shared goal that coincides with the company's vision of a desired future? What words will best inspire their efforts? Holding the vision, you consider the mix of skills and competencies that are now needed. Your honest appraisal and acceptance of who your team members are enables you to truly assist them in their development.

In addition, the intra-team relationships need to be strong. The following questions may guide your reflection and serve as talking points for a pre-project team meeting:

- What do you believe it will take for each person to be a strong contributor? Are skills missing on the team?

- What do you see as the team members' individual strengths and weaknesses?

- Can you separate grounded facts and performance evidence from your opinions about each person?

- How are individual perceptions about one another affecting the working relationships?

Keep in mind that there may be someone in a position that is a poor fit for his or her talents and skills. You may need to shift assignments to make the best use of everyone's skills. Employees with more likeable personalities may get away with things, while someone else is held to higher standards. All of these human issues surface in team environments and require strong observer muscles to sift through and differentiate between what is important from what is unimportant.

Intimately knowing your observer deepens and expands your self-awareness allowing you to be more personally disciplined and take more effective actions. The critical point to this discussion is to know who you are now, separate and distinct from the person you were five, ten, or twenty years ago. While your past has some influence on how you function in the present, it is not the sole arbiter. New information challenges your image of the old you. As you learn more about the current you, it is easier to see and accept yourself in the present. The connection is complete as you accept yourself, manage your behaviors, build upon your strengths, and rapidly accelerate your personal professional development.

Expanding your ability to observe and then understand how you filter your observations clearly benefits your personal and professional development as well as your interactions with others. Consider the case study below and then answer the questions that follow it.

CASE STUDY

Ellyn had worked really hard. Getting this promotion to project leader was the opportunity of a lifetime. When Tim announced he was leaving to take a VP spot in Boston, Ellyn was sad he was leaving and excited because she saw herself in contention for his job. And she got the job. Her company was a major player in the software development arena in Chicago. It was growing rapidly and she was now positioned to make a bigger contribution to its growth. Her head was spinning with ideas about how to create the software. She couldn't wait to show everyone her ideas at tomorrow's first project meeting.

When she called her best friend David to tell him her good news, he was not as happy for her as she would have hoped. He was worried about her and did not want her to relive his promotion nightmare. As he spoke she remembered the incident and how painful the transition had been for him. He had been at his company only a short time before the promotion, and several people felt overlooked and resented his success. He had trouble maintaining his managerial cool when conflicts broke out between sales reps.

Somehow he would get sucked into their arguments. They kept coming to him, wanting him to be judge and jury and end their petty squabbles. His decisions never won him friends. In the end the tension was so bad that it began to take a toll on his health and their relationship. They stayed friends, but David eventually found a new job in a new city.

As David talked, Ellyn began to think about her own situation. Her new team was really her old team. The only difference was she was in charge of an important software development project that would revolutionize how customers shopped online. How would they take to her as their manager? Were the congratulations she had been receiving sincere?

Ellyn made a quick phone call and headed out the door. She needed to think about what her approach should be at the morning meeting, and her former boss, now her mentor and confidant, was available and ready to serve as an objective sounding board.

Take on the role of Ellyn's mentor.

- What questions would you ask Ellyn to help her clarify what she wants to accomplish in her new position?

- What key points come to mind that you need to help Ellyn work through so that she embraces her new role as project leader as different from her old role as colleague?

- How can you effectively help Ellyn reveal assumptions and perceptions that could derail her efforts?

ACTIVITY: L-E-B Application

One of the points I always try to make with my coaching clients is that being offended or getting ticked off is a choice. Consider an event at work or in your personal life where you felt offended or felt resentment.

1. Draw the circles of the L-E-B model in a way that represents their positioning in this experience. Refer back to the model in Figure 2.2 if you need to refresh your memory of how the model works.

2. Think about how far you separate each circle from the others.

3. What is going on inside you—what is your inner voice saying that is causing each domain circle to be where you have drawn it?

4. Accepting that you are in the driver's seat of your life, the ultimate arbiter of all that is happening to you, consider what it will take to move the circles together thus empowering your actions. What must you do in the language domain, emotionally, and physically to let the offense pass through you and allow the circles to come together?

5. Take those actions over the next few days and note your results. Make adjustments as necessary to pull the circles together.

6. Once your actions pull the circle domains back together, what can you do to increase the size of the center space—that place where you take your most effective action?

ACTIVITY: Goal Reflection Cards

Research suggests that people who successfully set and achieve their goals experience greater satisfaction at work and in life. Introducing an introspective step facilitates goal accomplishment because it helps you stay focused. Use standard 3 x 5 cards and revisit your goal card at the end of each day to assess your progress. Be consistent with your practice.

1. Place one important goal on a card. List what you will have to do specifically to achieve this goal.

2. Incorporate elements of the L-E-B Model. Think about the language you must use when talking about this goal and planning your actions. What body presence will you need to develop to accomplish this goal? What emotional frame will you need to support your efforts?

3. Review your goal cards at the end of each day as part of your reflective practice. Notice how the domains of the L-E-B model worked together or separated. If they separated what caused it? What do you need to do to pull the domain back in ways that facilitate your achieving the goal?

Practice 3: Take Effective Action: Apply Focus and Choice

If you only have a hammer,
you tend to see every problem as a nail.
—Abraham Maslow

Where most other species are driven by instinct, human beings can act deliberately. Practice 3, taking effective actions, is about your ability to translate your intentions into purposeful actions that generate the results you want. Taking effective action lives in the public arena. What you do is visible, out there for all to see, and it builds on the two previous change practices—personal discipline and introspection—which totally exist in the private realm. You exert personal discipline to control what you are doing. Introspection allows you to consider the relationship between three critical intelligences (emotional, conceptual, and kinesthetic) and how each one is affecting your interpretations. Thus engaged, you can observe how you are translating emotional triggers and notice any physical signals your body may be sending. With discipline, you respond, choosing actions that bring you closer to your goals rather than reacting to what is before you, as is clearly shown in the continuum for practice 3.

You must constantly refine your own behaviors based on your growing insight to ensure that the actions you take produce the results you really want.

Knee-jerk
Reactions
(low)

Refined
Responses
(high)

Since doing is at the heart of taking effective action, the lone hammer cited in Maslow's quote above will no longer suffice. You need a full array of tools and techniques rooted in new learning about how you take action at your disposal. On the private side, understanding why you do what you do (practice 1) takes center stage. You learn how to sift through your deeper interpretations to recognize what will actually bring you closer to your overarching goals (practice 2). Once in the public arena, practice 3, the process piece, takes over. Taking effective action is all about employing new strategies to produce the desired end result.

Lights–Camera–Action

One way to learn how to take action is by paying attention to the examples around you. There are patterns that govern your actions in concert with the acceptable practices of your family, your heritage, your larger historical and religious communities, and the workplaces you join (Wilbur 1996). Many people identify with the common archetypes that show up in films and books: the hero, the protagonist, the victim, the martyr, the servant, the peacekeeper, the savior, to name a few. They try to emulate these archetypes to varying degrees of success. While a Rambo style might work in some situations, this character mode would be inappropriate and totally useless in other situations. Before moving on, give some thought to archetypes that you might copy. Which of these labels resonates for you?

The important point to recognize is that there are many action modalities open to you at any given point in time. Developing your change intelligence specifically means that you are embracing new practices to open up a more complete repertoire of action dispositions for your use. Figure 2.6 describes the five primary action dispositions—determination, openness, stability, flexibility, and centeredness—in the dance of effective action. Most people have a dominant mode, their go-to mode. To truly change your results in more powerful ways requires that you become adept at moving through all five dispositions (Newfield Network 2000).

Figure 2.6 Dance of Effective Action

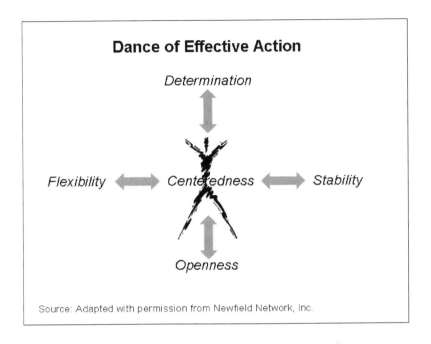

Dance of Effective Action

Determination

Flexibility   *Centeredness*   *Stability*

Openness

Source: Adapted with permission from Newfield Network, Inc.

Each of the five action dispositions has a mood, language, body stance, and emotional field. For example, determination is often represented by the warrior archetype and lives in a mood of confidence, ambition, and commitment. The language is "can-do," the body stance is strong, and the emotional field is powerful, energetic, and passionate about the desired goal. Stability is rooted and grounded. In this disposition, your body stance is firm, your language reassuring, your emotion steady and constant. Archetypes used to represent stability are kings or queens who become the rock of strength during troubling times. Think of flexibility as the magician. Lightness, joy, and possibility are the emotions with a body stance in motion, weaving and twisting with the winds, while keeping the focus on the goal. Openness is like floating in water. The archetype is the lover. The mood is tender, empathetic, totally accepting. You listen with heart, mind, and soul. And, finally, centeredness is about balance. All aspects of this disposition are calm and at peace.

Take a moment to consider each label and the language you might use when taking action from that disposition. What words come to mind? What emotions might you be experiencing in each position? What might your body feel like when you are determined, open, flexible, or stable? What does centered feel like? What do you do to get yourself into a centered, balanced space?

As I stated above, you are actually predisposed to take the actions that you are used to taking based on your disposition and experiences. There may be other actions that would serve you better, but your lack of familiarity with how these would feel stops you from even considering them. Think about what would happen to your results if you availed yourself of other possible action modalities?

Be forewarned. Each disposition also has a shadow side—a way of being that diminishes your effectiveness and could even sabotage your efforts. Think of the tyrants and dictators, evil villains and weaklings, clowns and court jesters that fill the pages of many stories. The shadow side of a disposition may show up as too much or too little. For example, a king quickly becomes a dictator when he is too forceful and controlling. Openness taken to an extreme can turn into impotence, addiction, weakness, and victimization, giving way to resignation and feelings of helplessness. Flexibility can become fantasy or give way to massive manipulation. Centeredness is easy when you come from a mindset of abundance but proves more difficult when you fear loss and you allow scarcity or greed to control your actions. The question to consider as you begin to take your first tentative dance steps is what type of language, emotion, and body do you need to create the life you want for yourself? Okay, yes, this is a big question!

Starting at a centered place is vital because you always have a choice about how you take action. Practice 1, exerting personal discipline, is your critical control lever. The key is to center yourself before you act each and every time, hence the use of the word *dance* in Figure 2.6. From center you are less likely to get pulled or hooked by others' actions. You remain in balance as their actions pass through you. Then, in full control, you step into the disposition you believe to be most appropriate, conduct the action, and step back to center. The pace of interactions makes this quite challenging, so learning how to move in this manner takes repeated practice. The fundamental goal of taking effective action is to learn to move—to dance—choosing the disposition most appropriate for any given situation.

One simple exercise to try follows the football workout known as chopping. Perhaps you have seen players moving their feet rapidly when you have driven by the local high school. To begin, stand with your feet squarely under your shoulders. Take a deep breath. Following the pattern of the diagram in Figure 2.6, step forward into determination with your right foot. Then move back to your starting position (centeredness). Take a deep breath. Now go to the right side (stability), return to center, breathe. Then step back (openness), return to center, breathe. Repeat using the left foot, moving to flexibility as you work around the left side of the image. Now that you have the idea, pick up the pace. Remember to take that all important centering breath each time you return to your starting position.

You can also practice some mental gymnastics to expand your thinking about each disposition in Figure 2.6. For example,

- If you are determined to make something happen, what words might you use? Can you think of a piece of music that expresses determination? What mood would inspire others and rally them to your cause? What emotion would best serve you when you are determined? What body stance? If you hold yourself to be a shy person and you are determined to accomplish a task, what words, emotion, and body stance would best serve you?

- What might flexibility look like physically? What music fits this disposition? What language?

- What words are used by someone who wants to express stability? Is there music that can play in your head that would support you when you want to act with stability?

- Would your arms crossed over your chest be a good stance for openness?

These dispositions flow and flex with one another. When your goal is to bring out the best in yourself and others, it is vital that you recognize and appreciate the energy fields in operation. Responding effectively and dancing with the energy produces the best results. Take the role of Tim as you read Claire's story. Think about how you might have better danced with Claire's energy.

Claire rushed into her manager Tim's office and blurted out her idea to improve service times at the drive-thru window. She was so excited. Her eyes were big and bright, almost on fire, wanting only his approval to get started. Tim sat calmly as Claire explained the process. He never moved an inch. His arms were relaxed on his desk and he just nodded as she explained what she envisioned. When Claire stopped, Tim asked his first question. Once answered, he had another, and another and yet another. All were delivered calmly and Claire answered every one. As she did, Claire could feel her energy and enthusiasm draining away. Why did she even bother? Tim was a details-only manager, and Claire was prepared to address his concerns, but he could have shown a little excitement. The air was let out of Claire's sails as she left Tim's office. Though he had given her the go-ahead, she knew she needed to hit her internal refresh button to reignite and galvanize her positive energy before proceeding.

Tim's lack of enthusiasm was like pouring water on Claire's passion. She had answers to his questions, which showed her awareness of his operating style. As her manager, however, Tim appeared blind to Claire's operating style. Can you think of language that Tim could have used to show appreciation for Claire's efforts and get his concerns handled? Now link your new learning about your predispositions for taking action with the L-E-B model. When Claire left Tim's office, what do you think was the position of her emotional domain? What language did she need her inner voice to use to fortify her and help her regroup? Can you see her shoulders slumping with each question Tim asked?

Recall the deer hunting example used in the earlier discussion. Let's change the scenario a bit, name the person Chris, and make you the manager. The conditions are the same; everyone is overworked. Chris is in front of you requesting time off. What do you do? What do you say? And yes, you do have choices here.

Your most important choice is about outcome: what outcome do you want to create? Your growing ability to think things through shows up here as does your ability to discipline and control your own actions, not letting any immediate emotional outburst derail your efforts. What message do you want to convey to Chris in both the short and long term and to everyone else who will know about the situation in a few minutes? Again, both the private and public domains intersect.

Internally, you begin by noticing your self-talk. What words are going through your head? What assessments and judgments are you making about Chris right now? Moving to the emotional and body domains, what emotions are you experiencing? Where do you notice tension in your body? Moving to the external, what outcome do you want to foster in the relationship with Chris and other employees who will be affected by this situation? What words support this outcome? What physical position does your body need to take to better ensure the outcome you want? How you move through the dispositions of determination, stability, openness, and flexibility with Chris right now will reveal a lot about how well you are using your emotional energy to create the results you really want.

In a time of drastic change, it is the learners
who inherit the future.
—Eric Hoffer

Effective Action Cycle: Focus–Choose–Act–Adjust

The good news is that there is a definable and learnable four-part process to help you take effective actions, which builds on the other change intelligence practices you've been learning. The four components of the effective action cycle—focus, choose, act, and adjust—reinforce and blend with one another (Figure 2.7). With consistent practice and repetition, this process will become seamless.

Figure 2.7 Take Effective Action Cycle

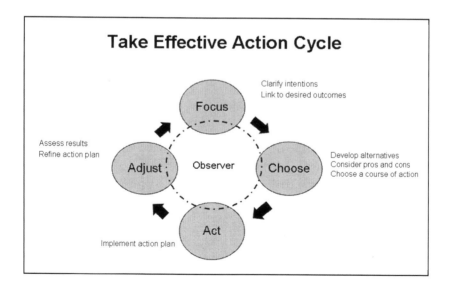

Focus. Focusing your intentions begins the process and might be considered the easiest component. Knowing what you want to accomplish would seem obvious considering the discussion so far. And yet, many times you only consider your wants and needs at a surface level. Probing deeper—connecting the dots around your intentions and desired outcomes—sharpens your actions. For example, consider a sales manager who wants to increase department sales by 10 percent. How can she get there? She knows that her main product line has several complimentary applications, and these "add on" sales would accomplish the goal. To make these sales though, she will need to leverage each client contact. With clarity about what she wants, she establishes the framework for her next steps.

Choose. Choosing your course commits you to a plan of action. It involves developing alternatives, evaluating the options, and then finally choosing a course of action. Because there are many ways to achieve what you want, it is important first to remove your judgment hat and allow your ideas to flow. Generate as many alternatives as you can that could deliver the results you want. In the example above, some alternatives might include brainstorming sessions to assess missed opportunities on calls. Scripting could become a tool to help the staff link ancillary products, while bundling applications could create attractive sales packages. The sales manager could also hold training sessions on how to handle the objections that her sales people might encounter. She could have sales people buddy up, or create mentoring opportunities for newer staff.

Once you have brainstormed possible alternatives, you will need to use your critical thinking skills to build a pro/con scenario for each option. Prioritize and determine how well each scenario fits your situation and could produce your desired goal, the 10 percent sales increase.

Now, at last, you are ready to choose your course. You commit to one course of action, letting go of the others.

Act. Once the choice is made, you take action. You do what you say you will do. Be deliberate. Apply your energy to whatever task moves you forward. Each action must align and connect to the results you want and should never be impulsive or reactionary. At times, you will act with precision in a logical sequence. At other times, you will zig and zag.

Two important elements impact the outcomes of this action step: managing your emotions and holding effective conversations. Let's take emotions first. You must make a concerted effort to work through any emotional triggers. Rather than locking them down, deal with what is showing up, and keep yourself focused on your desired future. Continuing with our sales example, team members may experience disappointment being paired with someone whose style does not mesh with their own. They may resent the idea of working with someone else altogether, not wanting to share sales techniques that have enabled them to earn top sales status. All of these scenarios could cause the emotional domains of some team members to implode, which on the outside reads as "attitude." Recognizing that future possibilities will open or close based on how they respond can help team members contain their immediate ego needs. They can choose to take the high road. They can see that their career interests are better served by being contributors and team players now.

The second key element in the action step revolves around the conversations you hold and those you don't. Because you don't live in a vacuum, consideration must be given to the people who are touched by your words, your choices, and your actions. The people at work and in your personal life are on the receiving end of you. The question you must consider is this: what are they receiving? Engaging in conversations is an inclusive act showing respect and honor for others. Each conversation you hold is unique to both purpose and person.

In conversation, you come face to face with the small promises you make in the moment. Continuing our example, the sales manager might promise to have the new sales script ready for the team to practice by day's end, but she doesn't get it done. Or perhaps she commits to a daily 9:00 a.m. pre-shift huddle to encourage everyone before their first calls, but consistently shows up late, disrespecting others and diminishing her own reputation. What kind of impact could this behavior have on her team? Because trust is at heart effective communication, keeping your word shows your trustworthiness and that you place a high value on your relationships with others. Even the simple action conversation, "I'll call you back in five minutes" has ramifications. Meaning what you say requires discipline on your part, especially when so many demands are tugging at you. Failure to follow through on small promises like these can easily derail your purpose and intentions and future career opportunities.

Beyond the small promises that you make, the larger job of focused conversations is to strengthen your relationships through clarity and openness and garner the support of your nuclear network (the people whose lives may change as you pursue your goals). Even your smallest goals may affect other people. During your conversations, you must clearly describe your expectations and clarify account-abilities as you see them. Openly discuss what you will do differently and how you see the work unfolding. Be open to how others are feeling and responding in the situation. What are their expectations and what changes are they willing to make to ensure the success of the work? Talk through concerns so that nothing is left unsaid. Ask for a specific verbal commitment from the people involved and maintain your relationships in conversations through-out the process.

Adjust. The last step in the action process cycle is to assess and adjust. As Lee Childs' character, Jack Reacher, said, "Plans go to hell as soon as the first shot is fired." Until there is action, you really do not know what will happen. Stay alert and be perceptive about the results you are obtaining while you are in an action mode. Based on the results you are getting, can you make adjustments in real time and change course when necessary? Being open as new possibilities emerge should become your modus operandi and is the fundamental change intelligence learning associated with practice 3. Assessing results in the moment and pivoting to more responsive actions is the power behind the flexibility disposition. Reassess and then respond, always keeping your goal front and center.

> *Success seems to be connected with action.*
> *Successful people keep moving.*
> *They make mistakes, but they don't quit.*
> —*Conrad Hilton*

Insights for Action

As with many of the topics here, taking effective actions has two parts: internal and external. Stephen Covey (1989) talked about this as the two acts of creation: 1) you see what you want in your mind, where you want to go, or what you want to have happen; and then 2) you take action, actually doing tasks to reach your target. The internal part is all about introspection, thinking things through and then disciplining yourself. You mentally and emotionally process your planned actions around your stated intentions. How you take action is the external part, visible for all to see. And, know this, others are watching, taking notes and making judgments about you based on what they observe.

Learning how to incorporate new possible responses to situations you encounter expands your opportunities. Thinking about the words you use, the emotions you exhibit, and how you carry yourself gives you action options. What actions are available to you? Which are outside your range of actions? How can you incorporate new moves in ways that serve you? When everything comes together, and your goals and desires reach fruition, you will look back and recognize just how far you have really come.

Follow your bliss and the universe will open doors for you where there were only walls.
— Joseph Campbell

CASE STUDY

Here is a story about Walter and Justin, two men whose careers converge at a time when both need to grow their change intelligence around the changes taking place at work. After reading through the case, answer the questions based on what you believe you would do in each situation.

Walter was the corporate fixer, the person brought in to turn store operations around. His approach was aggressive, and he got results. He told people what to do, the problem got fixed, and Walter moved on to the next store. Because he never stayed long in one location, his brashness and explosive tendencies were tolerated. He developed callousness about relationships, driven to action by the numbers. His commanding style was supported by his physical presence, a tall man who moved purposefully and fast. Walter's reward was a promotion to regional manager of his own territory. This new role required practices completely different from those that landed him the promotion.

Justin, a high-producing and motivated manager, was excited about a new store layout he'd designed to increase complimentary sales. He enthusiastically shared his ideas with Walter at their regular weekly meeting. When Justin finished, Walter pounced on him, still incensed that Justin had left his presentation a week earlier. Justin, flustered and almost speechless, explained that his leaving was related to an emergency at his store. Justin left his meeting with Walter feeling angry and defensive. As he pondered his unexpected "dressing down," he realized that Walter had not once addressed his new idea. Walter's actions had left Justin feeling completely deflated and his excitement for the new store layout was gone.

Walter had held onto his anger about Justin's departure the previous week, which fueled his actions during the weekly meeting. In his past role, no one dared walk out when he was talking. His previous experiences had left him unprepared for the managerial challenges he was facing—an intact team and accomplishing goals through others. His reaction showed an insensitivity and failure to fully appreciate how he treated people.

Imagine you are Walter's manager and you witnessed Justin leaving the large presentation. The grapevine works well in your company, and you also heard rumors about what transpired during Walter's meeting with Justin. Consider your next step:

- How could you coach Walter using the dispositions in the Dance of Effective Action graphic to learn new words, emotions, and body stances that would better serve his interactions in his new role?

- What questions would you ask Walter to help him see his own behaviors?

Now imagine that you are Justin's best friend at work. You are sharing beers after work and Justin tells you what happened and asks for your advice. Staying with the five dispositions of action—determination, openness, stability, flexibility, and centeredness—what advice do you offer to Justin?

ACTIVITY: Dancing with Effective Actions

Take a recent situation from work. Practice some mental gymnastics as you relive the details. Use the Dance of Effective Action graphic as a guide.

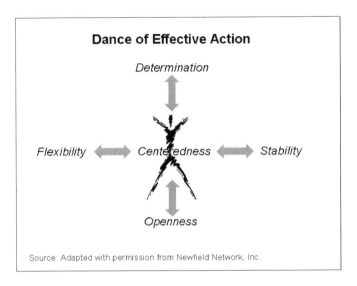

Dance of Effective Action

Determination

Flexibility ⟷ *Centeredness* ⟷ *Stability*

Openness

Source: Adapted with permission from Newfield Network, Inc.

- What were you determined to accomplish?

    - Did your language support you or diminish your effectiveness?

    - What mood/emotion were you revealing to others as you talked about your goal?

- How did you use each of the five dispositions for action to your advantage?

    - How did you show you were flexible?

    - Was there a need for you to show yourself as stable (trustworthy) during the situation?

    - How did you express openness to others during the situation?

- Reviewing the situation now, what are you seeing that you did not see in the heat of the moment?

  - Did the shadow side of your actions pay you a visit during the event?

  - Did you show frustration or cut people off when they were sharing an idea?

- Did you manipulate anyone in any way?

- In hindsight, how could you have handled the entire situation more effectively?

- What new learning can you take away that will serve you well next time?

3

Building Synergy for the "We" Organization

*If you want to build a ship, don't herd people together
to collect wood and don't be so rigid to assign tasks and work,
but rather teach them to long for the immensity of the sea.*
— *Antoine de Saint-Espery*

The change intelligence factor is the power you develop as you integrate the three change practices we have been exploring— exerting personal discipline, cultivating introspection, and taking more effective action. As you ground your actions and apply these higher order practices, you become more able to meet the challenge of the "we" organization, that is, an organization with an exceptional level of synergistic collaboration.

Creating the environment where a "we" organization can flourish is not magic. Like any new initiative, it is valuable to envision it first. Imagine a place where participants bring their best efforts to the work, where people are excited about their projects and focus their energies more on how they can contribute than on getting credit. Imagine an environment where people are honored, everyone's ideas are valued, and rewards are shared equally. Finally, imagine a place where people have fun and experience real joy in creating something new. To these imaginings, most people would say, "Count me in!" And that is precisely what needs to happen.

In this chapter, I will introduce the "we" organization and then present four applications that will help you build synergy for this kind of effective, strong organization. The four applications include becoming engagement centric, harnessing the power of conversation, embracing the possibility of conflict, and leading/serving. Integrating the practices you have been learning here is foundational to mastering change intelligence.

You must be strong as an individual actor so that you become an effective contributor to the larger organization.
—*Jane R. Flagello*

The process begins when you reconstitute how you see your relationship with any organization you join. Regardless of your designated position, your efforts must foster an environment that embraces change as a catalyst to generate opportunities for mutually beneficial outcomes. There is no "they." *Everyone* owns this responsibility, which is a major difference from the way most workplace environments work. An examination of the work you do and the sense of ownership, meaning, and fulfillment you derive from your work might require more probing on your part. Balancing and adjusting the risk–reward equation proves useful. For example, giving a project your all only to be rewarded with less than what you consider to be fair by people who are at the same time making sure their own pockets are overflowing belies the realities of how organizations can best compete on an interdependent global stage. Aspirational appeals only work when followed up with policies perceived as balanced and fair by members of the community.

Here are a few starter questions to open your exploration:

- How do I effectively utilize newfound emotional, cognitive, and kinesthetic intelligence capabilities in my work, interactions, and relationships?

- How do I foster a workplace environment that generates commitment and engages the creative energies of everyone?

- How do I build influence and lead in more powerful ways?

- What do I need to do differently to manage the processes and lead employees so that we all can innovate and deliver products and services with uncompromising excellence to people eager to become loyal customers and ready to sing our praises?

> *Alone we can do so little; together we can do so much.*
> *—Helen Keller*

Introducing the "We" Workplace

How does it feel to work here? is the most important question to ask when attempting to create the environment within which synergy thrives. There is an energy that inspires and motivates as people gain a stronger appreciation for how their efforts align and add value to the larger whole. The senior management of the organization plays a huge role in establishing your workplace environment. Management traditionally sets the tone and creates the rules of engagement, both by its words and through its actions. How well your management group is doing at this task is evident from the results being achieved and the answers employees give to the opening question.

I firmly believe that you have a role to play in setting the tone that supports the environment you want to experience, regardless of whether you are the CEO, a mid-level manager, or a front-line employee. Embrace the challenge to create what you want. This is not a naïve suggestion. What would happen if your efforts to create a highly effective, collaborative environment were adopted by other departments and project teams? It could be that what you do to foster a "we" environment might just become the collaborative standard for the larger organization.

Keep the *How does it feel to work here?* question in your mind as you consider each element in Figure 3.1. Your behaviors contribute directly to the environment that is created as do the behaviors of your colleagues. Five key components constitute a "we" organization: community, trust, perspective, learning, and commitment. Your thoughts about these components inform the actions that you take. They are fed from the well of your personal character. Your perspective, your capacity for learning, and your ability to make and keep your commitments feed into and nurture the larger community environment. All are crucial elements for a collaborative workplace. And your growing change intelligence will serve you well as you make internal changes that support a more synergistic organization.

Figure 3.1 Synergy of "We"

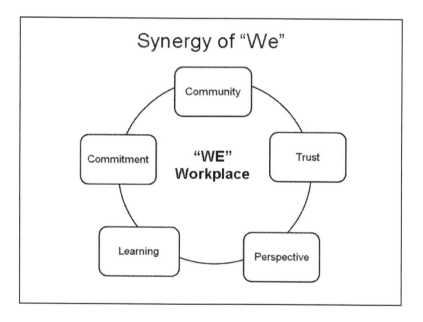

Community

Community means relationships. Strong communities have both written and unwritten shared values. These tenets guide everyone's behaviors and interactions, infusing a sense of purpose and ownership. Community emanates from a sense of service—that each one is doing important work that offers meaning beyond a paycheck. It also emanates from a sense of safety; people can speak their truth, take risks, share opinions, and not fear reprisals or negative ramifications down the road. Community thrives when everyone truly cares about one another in a way that manifests in each and every interaction. Divergent points of view are respected for what they really are: opportunities to tap into the creative wisdom of all participants. Attention is equally focused on making progress to meet project goals and maintaining relationships among the people involved. High levels of collegial respect breed openness, inclusivity, and integrity.

Clearly, what is being described here encompasses more than wearing marketing logos on clothing and conducting team-building activities. *How does it feel to work here? What words do people use during their interactions? What is the emotional temperature?* Where community lives, the investment is in the people. Conversations are positive, filled with praise for others and stories of work well done. Feedback replaces criticism because its tone is suggestive; its goal is only to make things better.

Trust

Trust is the currency of all relationships. Your ability to dance with what shows up, be flexible, and respond to people and events is trust sensitive. When trust is high, the dance flows. When trust is low, everyone steps on one another's toes. Cultivating mutual respect, keeping commitments, extending dignity, and providing satisfying experiences are the fertile soil within which trust grows. With every memo, interaction, and touch point, employees assess your credibility, integrity, and trustworthiness, as you, in turn, assess theirs.

Trust in this context is a grounded assessment. You make it in the present, but it is predicated on your past interactions and experiences with these people. Your assessment then informs your future relationships. You make an internal decision about whether to extend trust freely, guardedly, or withhold it completely.

Do you trust the people you work with? Do you think they trust you? Are your actions trustworthy? Are theirs? On the continuum of trust levels that follows, consider where you might place the people with whom you have relationships or people in your nuclear network? What criteria are you using in your trust assessment and is it the same for everyone? Some of the more common trust elements include reliability, sincerity, and competence. Do these terms resonate for you as you make your assessments? How do you fare when you assess yourself using these criteria? How well do your actions match your words? Do you consistently extend genuine respect to employees and co-workers even when they are not present?

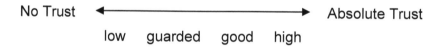

No Trust ⟵——————————————⟶ Absolute Trust

low   guarded   good   high

Going one step further, consider a situation where you are face to face with each person you are now assessing on the trust continuum above. How would you complete the following statement? *The most important thing you can do to build trust with me is* _____. I've used this activity in many workshops, and while it does place people in vulnerable positions, I've received feedback that the activity invites more powerful conversations after the workshop ends. Participants have told me that their relationships with some peers have dramatically changed for the better.

Perspective

How you see the world and how you see yourself within that world are the dual aspects of perspective. To produce synergy, you need to show up with a mindset of abundance. There is more than enough for everyone. You come to the work as one among many. And herein lives a primary tension. What is required is a "we" and not a "me" internal narrative. You manage your ego and your preconceived notions of how things should unfold. You adopt a philosophical belief that your colleagues are competent, add value, will carry their share of the work load, and are aligned around the same vision and project goals as you are. You have to embrace openness and become a contributor, not just a participant. You stay focused on the goal or desired result and are flexible with the process of how to reach it. You share your point of view in ways that support forward movement and invite competing perspectives. And you practice patience with colleagues until they get to the same place you are.

Learning

The "we" workplace is all about learning. And you must learn how to become a willing, hungry learner. Beyond skill development, learning encompasses your ability to grow. Ignited by curiosity, you actively seek out new information that expands your understanding of events and people. The state of not knowing is your starting point. As you begin to know, what is it in your language, emotion, and body that reflect your newfound knowing? In addition to your technical competence, your relationship abilities will be put to the test. Multigenerational and multicultural understanding is important. You will find that your emotional domain and your physical domain get quite a workout. Are they up to the task? Consider these domains your early warning system that trouble may be about to pay you a visit. Deliberate action is required to maintain your composure, keep your personal needs and ego in check, open yourself to truly listen, and stay focused on learning.

Commitment

Commitment focuses on your ability to hold yourself accountable. Included here is your ability to deliver on the promises you make, to speak your truth, and to own your outcomes. Rooted in the emotional domain, the day-to-day agreements and promises you make to yourself and others, and then keep or break, create your relationships. Your real actions shape others' assessments about whether to trust you, whether they can depend on you. Trust means that when someone is depending upon you, you deliver as promised, or you renegotiate the promise before it is due.

Commitments are challenged by breakdowns. Something has happened that stops you in your tracks. It's an *"Oh, shit"* moment, and those two little words, uttered out loud or between your ears, signal its presence. Your forward movement is stopped. Whatever commitment you have made to someone else, or to yourself, is not going to be fulfilled. Breakdown! Your next action here seems obvious, but if you are the cause of the breakdown it may be difficult to do. Communicate with anyone and everyone involved, tell them what has happened and renegotiate your commitment. There is no room for blame, no space for recriminations. Take responsibility and take action to maintain trust or rebuild it if necessary.

> *When people honor each other, there is a trust established that leads to synergy, interdependence, and deep respect.*
> —Blaine Lee

Insights for Action

The turbulence of our modern workplace provides us with many challenges and opportunities that often present themselves as intractable problems. Many such problems represent the breakdowns of the modern age: failures to communicate, lead, take responsibility for our own actions, and generously contribute without concern about who gets the credit. And each breakdown presents you with the possibility of showing how extra-ordinary you are. Embrace these as magical moments, learning opportunities, ripe with possibility to strike out on new adventures.

The bottom line is that the "we" workplace harvests the wisdom of a cooperative of talented people who bring out the best in one another to achieve remarkable results. Breakdowns are reimagined as opportunities for all. This workplace thrives with authentic leadership. It advocates for a higher level of collaboration, one that requires a good fit of personal competencies to the goals of the project, and a commitment that surpasses hidden agendas and individual gain.

Human beings, by changing the inner attitudes of their minds,
can change the outer aspects of their lives.
—William James

ACTIVITY: Assessing Your "We" Capabilities

Your alignment as a whole person—in thought, word, and deed—signifies you as worthy to participate in a "we" organization. Take some time now to assess your "we" capabilities. Use the questions below and think about a recent project. Keep in mind that your memory is only an interpretation of your experience, colored by your perceptions and shaded by time.

- Which of your actions promote forward progress and synergy? Which actions stymie it?

- What factors must be in place for you to contribute your best?

- When you run into roadblocks or breakdowns during a project, what seems to be their cause? Are these breakdowns outside of your control or of your creation?

- What self-managing problems do you experience? Where do you observe others struggling with their own personal discipline gremlins?

Application 1: Become Engagement Centric

*If we did the things we were capable of
we would astound ourselves.*
—Thomas Edison

There is no getting around this simple truth: strong relationships and meaningful work are the secret ingredients to creating an engaging organization, and emotional investment is the glue. Job satisfaction is fine as far as it goes. It supports the employer–employee contract—a job well done—both parties pleased with the results. Unfortunately, job satisfaction—just being satisfied—rarely ignites the creative juices, ingenuity, and innovative spirit that motivate and drive people to go above and beyond, which is the essence of engagement.

To create a truly engaged, high-performing organization, each employee must see the work as energizing and stimulating. When employees believe their efforts are meaningful, when they feel heard, and when they perceive opportunities to learn and advance, their best performance is naturally generated. Engaged people embrace the work itself because it challenges them and allows them to apply their gifts. Excited about their contributions, they see themselves as important to the outcome. They also enjoy one another and the relationships that connect their hearts. What I am describing is all about perceptual context, and it is conceived and strengthened one person at a time, with each interaction.

For this discussion, engagement is defined as the complete connection and commitment of heart, mind, body, and soul made by each individual employee that fuels the delivery of their best performance. Engaged employees own their work. Like Stephen Covey's (2004) description of the whole person paradigm, engaged employees approach their work with dedication and positive, focused energy. The work itself becomes the propellant that pulls them in and keeps them connected. They become engrossed with what "is" as their minds race with the possibility of what "could be."

Figure 3.2 Engagement-Centric Space

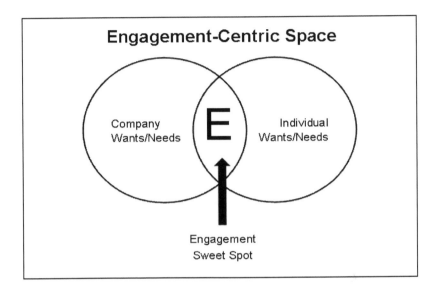

Everyone brings his or her needs to work. The engagement sweet spot is that space where company needs/wants and employee needs/wants mesh as shown in Figure 3.2. Engaged employees ignite their motivation and creativity genes in ways that elevate their conversations, improving the work and producing amazing products and outstanding services. The catalyst is their sense of belonging, being part of something important. They are partners with their employers, and together they create a community. Reciprocity between engaged employees and their organizations means that they are fully committed to their work and their companies are fully committed to them and their well-being.

The conversations that engaged employees hold are different because of how they truly value their relationships with one another. Finding solutions to problems is important; the relationship between people is equally important. Each person's full participation strengthens and deepens these relationships. There is a seamless flow between problem solving and relatedness, with each component making the other stronger.

You may be thinking it is management's job to create the environment described above. After all, we expect management to set the company's direction, develop goals, clarify work expectations, write the policies, provide the tools to support the work, and control the purse strings when it comes to rewards. If you are a member of management, you do exert influence over each individual employee's engagement choice in both subtle and dramatic ways.

The key to evoking engaged performance, however, goes deeper than just what management does and says. It requires more than trotting out the old cliché that people are the most important assets. The critical distinction being made here is that no matter where you find yourself on the organizational structure chart, you have a role to play in creating an engagement-centric environment. Being engaged, or not, is a choice made by each individual. Examining the actions that everyone brings to work, who each person is being in addition to the work each person is doing, sets apart an engaged person from the rest. And this choice is reinforced or degraded by the thousands of things that get done to create and sustain the commitment, passion, and pride of these people. It's doing business, or whatever it is we are doing, with all of our faculties fully engaged—our heads, our hearts, and our souls.

> *The new workplace will be one of*
> *shared aspirations, empowered*
> *employees at all levels and creativity. It*
> *will be fast, focused, flexible, and*
> *friendly. It will also be fun.*
> *—Rosabeth Moss Kanter*

Putting engagement at the heart of our organizations, with all of its synergies and benefits, seems like a no-brainer. Who wouldn't want to work for such an organization? So why do so few companies function like this? The answer is simple. Fostering this kind of engagement in light of the many forces working against it (apathy, burnout, bad policies, resistance to change, and so on) can seem daunting. To assist you in this task, I offer several tools and strategies to help you foster engagement in your professional life and in your organizations, including benchmarking best practices, building strong relationships, employing engaging questions, and addressing the unengaged.

Benchmarking Best Practices in Engagement

The level of relationships required to truly engage people flows from a deep understanding of how people make and keep commitments with one another, with you, and with their companies. Demanding more than a clear vision, engagement sets and honors boundaries, clarifies expectations, and manages perceptions and outcomes. It supports those difficult conversations that clear the path for everyone to coordinate their actions to achieve mutually agreed-on goals. Your authenticity opens the space to share feelings, thoughts, and ideas, which is where engagement really happens.

The list in Figure 3.3 can serve as a benchmark of habits and practices of engaged people.

Figure 3.3 Rate Your Engagement

Start with yourself. Rate how strongly you agree or disagree with the engagement best practices listed. Strong agreement indicates you are highly engaged; weak or no agreement means low engagement.

- **You "get over it."** You don't take things personally and can let go of slights, offenses, and other things that prevent you from doing what needs to be done in the present moment to move forward.

Strongly Disagree	*Strongly Agree*
Low Engagement	**High Engagement**

- **You operate from what you want to see happen.** You are highly connected to your vision of what's possible. This drives you forward toward desired results, regardless of what others around you are doing.

Strongly Disagree	*Strongly Agree*
Low Engagement	**High Engagement**

- **You create adult relationships.** You treat everyone with dignity and respect. You perceive management, not as a benevolent dictator or parent, but as a partner in work operations.

Strongly Disagree	*Strongly Agree*
Low Engagement	**High Engagement**

- **You feel empowered to take risks and accept the consequences of even your toughest decisions.**

Strongly Disagree	*Strongly Agree*
Low Engagement	**High Engagement**

- **Being creative, your curiosity energizes your actions.** You want to be doing what you are doing.

Strongly Disagree	*Strongly Agree*
Low Engagement	**High Engagement**

- **You are a learner.** You strive to develop and improve seeking out new techniques to try. You accept being questioned, evaluated, or judged as a learning opportunity and a chance to grow. Feedback is your ally because it helps you become your best.

Strongly Disagree	*Strongly Agree*
Low Engagement	**High Engagement**

And since relationships with colleagues play a pivotal role in engagement, think about your co-workers, members of your team, your department, and your company as a whole. Can you find these habits in those you consider to be highly engaged? Can these practices help you open up a conversation with those who need help?

The groundwork you need to become more engaged with your work and to create an engagement-centric organization has already been established. Our discussions to this point outlined the playing field, proposing three critical practices—exerting personal discipline, thinking things through, and taking effective action to enhance your change intelligence factor capabilities. With these practices as your foundation, your actions draw on their strength and power.

Now, the job is to operationalize these points, to offer examples and change intelligence strategies so that you can shift your reactions into responses that enable your best performance to emerge. Consider the following list of behaviors that cultivate engagement-centric organizations as a standard to measure against and strive to achieve. And if, as you review the bullets, you realize that achieving an engagement-centric environment is hard work, you are absolutely right. The principle behaviors of engagement-centric organization include:

- Employees listen to one another without interruption because this is the only way to respect and honor one another.

- There is no perceived need to fix people, only to create a space where people feel safe and where there is a high level of prudent trust.

- Ideas shared are valued without judgment.

- Participation and conversations are open and designed to generate something new.

- Each interaction builds community, and each person believes this to be an important part of his or her job.

Take a few minutes now to assess your own behaviors during a recent meeting or interaction. Review each point above as you replay the encounter in your mind. Become conscious of yourself in action mode. Think about both your outward actions and your inner voice. After all, your self-talk has the uncanny ability to sabotage your best intentions. Were your actions building collaborative energy or were you cutting people off to get your points across? What emotional field was in charge? How was your mood energy impacting your actions and the actions of others? Were your contributions creating the results you wanted?

> *Treat people as if they were what they ought*
> *to be and you help them to become*
> *what they are capable of being.*
> —*Johann Wolfgang von Goethe*

Building Relationships That Engage

Workplaces are relationship places. There is a tremendous body of research ranging from Mary Parker Follett's organizational development work in the early twentieth century to present day that supports the importance of the relationships in engaged workplaces. Just Google employee engagement and you will receive thousands of hits describing resources, survey results, courses, and books all designed to help you develop an engaged workplace. The distinction I am making here is that you are the primary actor in the engagement process. Therefore, your underlying goal must be to learn how to build relationships that enable employees to "partner" so that they will make and keep workplace commitments, which, in turn, lead to producing extra-ordinary results.

Continuing the premise of a private to public shift, the learning goal is to uncover ways of being that foster an engagement-centric environment, first at a personal level and then as a member of the larger team. Engagement is all about how it feels to be in this relationship. Think about it. You interact with all sorts of people on a regular basis. You rarely ever just have a great or terrible relationship with someone. Connections between people move along a continuum from good to bad, strong to weak, trust to distrust.

Your relationship with a person emerges and changes with each encounter. The dynamics are usually centered on everyone getting his or her needs met. When both of you get what you want from the encounter, the relationship flourishes. When you don't, interactions may feel strained or awkward. This is the essence of the emotional bank account that Stephen Covey (1989) talked about in *7 Habits of Highly Effective People*.

As you develop your change intelligence, you become more attuned to the ebb and flow of each interaction and can more astutely recognize the effect of each encounter. Self-awareness places you in control of your actions allowing you to make more effective choices about what to do and say. You expand your authentic influence, regardless of your designed role and title within the organization. As before, questions offer a starting point:

- What specific actions must I stop or start doing to create a space where colleagues can engage effectively with one another?

- What beliefs do I hold about my colleagues that serve our collaboration? Conversely, what beliefs detract from the collaboration?

- How well do I encourage people to connect with others to develop the best solutions?

- How can I help each person grow and become a contributing member of the team?

To help you explore what this looks like in practice, read Ian's story below and put yourself in his shoes. Think about what actions you would take in the same situation.

Ian stopped talking. Brad had just interrupted him for the third time during the meeting. There was a problem with the software and the group was brainstorming ways to fix the bug. Ian had spent the weekend figuring out a possible solution that seemed to have promise, if he could finish explaining it. Brad's ego needs were getting the best of him, again. No one was making eye contact around the table. Most had grown to accept Brad's behavior as "Brad being Brad." It was getting worse lately. After the last meeting, Ian had made a conscious decision to stop talking whenever Brad interrupted him. Looking around the table Ian sensed that everyone seemed to be totally disconnected from the discussion. The cost for tolerating Brad's behavior was getting higher with each meeting. This was a smart, talented group of software designers, and they were stopped cold by a guy who did not know how to play well with others. In the end, nothing got done. Their beta test customers continued to struggle and were left with quick fixes that did not work over the long term. Solutions were hit or miss, and the team's lack of commitment was evident to anyone who took the time to look. How could one individual do so much damage? More important, what could Ian do about it, and at this point, did he care enough to risk it?

In the scenario above, Brad's behaviors were damaging the relationships he had with his co-workers, who were disengaging because of his actions. Did he know? Did he care? What was missing for Brad that caused his behaviors? Could he have gotten his needs (attention, recognition) met in a more productive way? No one appeared motivated to have a conversation with Brad about his behaviors. What motives might have been behind the decisions not to get involved? If any members of the group expressed concerns to management, those concerns were either not shared with Brad or they were shared in a way that Brad could ignore. The meetings were unproductive and unsatisfying for all concerned, not to mention costly for the company.

Remember, everyone brings his or her needs to work. If you are the manager, you have to differentiate every individual's wants and needs and find ways to align them with the strategic needs of your organization in creative ways that encourage engagement (the sweet spot in Figure 3.2). As a team member, you need to support others, helping them achieve their needs as they in turn support you as you get your needs met. If and when you realize that you have taken more than you have given, you need to harness your courage and do what is necessary to reconnect and make the relationships work again.

The bottom line is that engagement is driven by how each person mentally envisions everyone else. It's all about relationships—the ties that bind us, build connections, and enable us to authentically commit to one another first (yes first) and then to the work. Everyone develops patterns of interactions that form their relationships. And these relationships (positive and supportive, or negative and undermining) are always present and set the tone for exactly how the work gets done, how productive you are, and how enjoyable you are to work with. When you perceive your peers, managers, and leaders as valuable contributing partners, you connect to their mind and spirit, as well as their muscle. You do this from the heart, guided by strong core values like honor, integrity, dignity, mutual respect, and trust.

We spend more time at work than we do with our family or friends. Yet we leave much of our passion, energy, and creativity at home. If we can't bring the best of ourselves to our work, we're saying it's okay to be unhappy, bored, or resigned for a big part of our lives.
—David Whyte

Employing Questions That Engage

One way to tap into the power of an engagement-centric workplace is to learn how to ask powerful questions. Questions are amazing! They are compelling tools because they invite others to join the conversation. *You want my input? You're asking me?* The key is to ask the right question, the right way, at just the right time.

Great questions—those that are open ended and thought provoking—allow the conversation that wants to happen to emerge. Questions extract wisdom. Questions build trust by evoking a sense of inclusion and respect on the part of the people being asked.

Reflect on your own questioning prowess for a moment. *Are your questions open ended and evoking, or closed and leading in a manipulative way?* The desired outcome from your questions is to have employees share their thoughts; not just give a "yes" or a "no" answer or their best guess of what they think you may want to hear. And let's be candid here. When you can handle people giving you honest input, rather than what they think you want to hear, you are truly engaging. Conversely, the decision not to invite questions is disengaging and self-limiting.

Questioning strategy engages people and supports contributions. Figure 3.4 highlights two pairs of reciprocal questions that hold tremendous power. At first blush they seem simple and obvious. Asking them actually demonstrates the power of a synergistic and collaborative workplace. Once asked, these questions change you from uninvolved bystander to engaged actor. As answers emerge in the space of the question, the way forward becomes clear. You are presented with choices—possible responses, commitment levels, and accountability decisions. Develop the routine practice of asking these powerful pairs of questions silently to yourself and out loud.

Figure 3.4 Questions That Engage

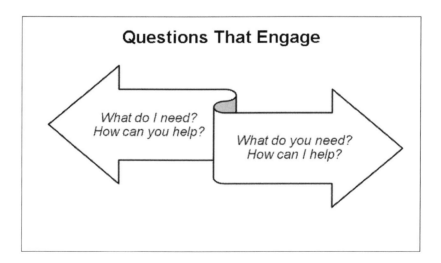

To help you appreciate the power of these questions, think about a current issue or situation on the job. Utilizing introspection and self-discipline, quiet your racing thoughts and ask yourself: *What do I need?* As obvious answers pop into your head, ask it again, and then again. Allow your full need to emerge from the clutter and chaos of your mind. And trust me, it will! Once revealed, you gain clarity about what is really happening. Now you can ask the question: *How can you help?* The "you" in this question could be any number of people: your staff, suppliers, customers, anyone who has a stake in the outcome of the situation. You can now invite action in ways that really will serve.

Move on to the second pair of questions. *What do you need?* invites conversations with others. It might take some time during the exchange of information that follows for needs to be revealed. Asking the question itself shows a level of care and concern that is part of the relationship-building process.

Asking *How can I help?* might seem unfamiliar at first. If you are a manager or team leader or co-worker, putting yourself out there and having the courage to ask this question might conjure up fears that you won't really have an answer or be able to provide the help requested. There may not be a quick solution. And it is certainly acceptable to say that you don't know. This admission exposes your humanness and strengthens opportunities for collaborating. It also presents the opportunity for someone else's leadership to emerge.

> *Our deepest calling is to grow into our own*
> *authentic self-hood, whether or not it conforms*
> *to some image of who we ought to be.*
> *As we do so, we will not only find the joy*
> *that every human being seeks—we will also*
> *find our path of authentic service in the world.*
> *—Parker J. Palmer*

Addressing the Unengaged

Building strong relationships and using artful questioning are effective strategies to create an engaging workplace, but one additional point must be addressed. It is a simple fact that unengaged employees work alongside engaged employees. The primary goal of the disengaged is to show up for work to collect a paycheck and do just enough to avoid getting reprimanded or fired.

You can recognize disengaged employees and colleagues through both subtle and conspicuous behaviors. Some disengaged people remain aloof; they exclude themselves from relationships with others. They avoid collaborative conversations and participate in meetings with closed body presence, silence, or noncommittal responses. Their apathy demonstrates limited motivation and a detachment that often produces mediocre work.

Other disengaged employees might demonstrate more challenging behaviors. They may focus their energies on complaining and criticizing rather than on productive efforts or problem solving. They may show up as snipers and saboteurs. And because misery loves company, this type of disengaged person might solicit allies for spreading negativity, sarcasm, and cynicism, all of which undermine morale.

Because disengagement flourishes in a closed, uninviting atmosphere, the first place to look for potential trouble signs breeding disengagement is the organization's culture. Remember, the culture supports the status quo. Are your employees or colleagues told both what to do and how to do it? Are they discouraged from questioning that formula? Do exchanges happen on a need-to-know basis, without listening to input from others, open sharing, or collaboration? Answering "yes" to these questions supports the old paradigm of hiring just "a body" to do the tasks of the job. It is an attitude of "don't think—just do what you are told." It is about directing, not evoking. It is from force, not freedom, that you create dependents. And if this sounds outrageous, do not be fooled into thinking that this management style or workplace environment no longer exists. There are departments in many organizations where managers are operating from this model and wondering why they are not getting the innovative solutions they claim to want and desperately need to be able to compete effectively.

Decisive action is a must in these situations. Peers can play an important role, perhaps more important because they are considered equals. Whether as manager or colleague, you can initiate conversations with people who you believe are not engaged. Uncover any possible reasons for disengagement, such as missing skills or competencies, emotional detachment, unchallenging work, or problems outside the organization that could be impacting the person. Use your interpersonal skills to connect on a level that makes this discussion productive. While not an easy task, it is essential and shows a level of caring that yields huge payoff for all concerned.

We cannot live for ourselves alone.
Our lives are connected by a thousand invisible threads,
and along these sympathetic fibers,
our actions run as causes and return to us as results.
—*Herman Melville*

Insights for Action

One of my favorite quotes is from Mr. Spock, the character from *Star Trek*. During a routine training mission that turned into a major crisis requiring the Starship *Enterprise* to save the day, Captain Kirk asks Spock how the new cadets will do. His answer is priceless: "*Each according to his gifts.*" The heart of an engagement-centric workplace beats through the willing contribution of our gifts. When we honor the talents of others as complements to our own, we create the space for truly extra-ordinary results. Together, all of our gifts make magic. This is the synergy for which we all strive.

ACTIVITY: Engage Now!

When you begin your next project or assignment, bring your team together for a meeting. Employ these engagement techniques and watch how they impact your team and its work.

1. Post the goals you have been assigned to achieve where everyone can see them. Knowing what is expected before starting will focus everyone's attention.

2. Open up the conversation for further exploration.

3. Clarify any aspects of the task that may be confusing.

4. Answer questions people may have about the assignment, its inherent and perceived challenges, and any other issues that will impact its completion.

5. Ask each member of your team to think about the task and his or her own unique skill set.

6. Finish up by asking each person to let you know how he or she will contribute to the required goal. Don't require an immediate response. Offer time so they can talk among themselves about the project, think about the challenges involved, and make a choice about what they want their role to be.

If your experience is anything like mine with this process, you will be surprised and delighted, with what follows. When given the opportunity people will rise to the challenge. Most people want to grow, to learn new skills, and to be part of something important. And when you choose what role you want to play and how you want to contribute, your commitment to producing extra-ordinary outcomes is almost always assured.

ACTIVITY: Go Viral!

Create a contagion of valued contributions. Valuing the contributions of others builds community and fuels engagement. We all want to know that what we do matters. I firmly believe that a significant portion of the adult population is starved for affirmation. When we don't acknowledge the value and contributions of others, we deny their greatness as well as our own. What would happen if you took the lead and made an active decision to notice the work of someone else and express how it specifically added value? Step up to the challenge. Look for opportunities to let others know how their efforts made a difference.

Here is the process:

1. Start with the person's name and make strong eye contact.

2. Be specific about the action, link it to the person's unique gift or talent, and how the action generated what was needed to make the contribution special.

3. Be genuine and sincere.

Spread the virus of valued contributions far and wide. And while the person may make a self-deprecating comment because he or she is momentarily embarrassed or caught off guard, trust me, deep down where it matters, the person will be warmed that you noticed his or her efforts. Move on the next day. Notice how long it takes for your actions to go viral—for others to follow your lead in acknowledging the contributions of their peers.

When we can generously tell other people how much they add to the situation, the work, our lives, in a way that makes them feel special, we exponentially increase the strength of their contributions. And remember, what goes around comes around.

CASE STUDY

Advances in technology and online security, along with efforts to reduce costs, moved Tom's company to develop systems where clients would do many transactions online at its web site. Management's rationale was to free account managers from routine tasks, allowing them to focus on adding real value during face-to-face meetings with clients. Unfortunately, at a time when staying close to customers seemed more crucial than ever, the sales team perceived management's actions differently. They saw the new initiatives as destructive to the relationships they had nurtured with customers.

As a leader on the sales team, Tom saw morale slowly deteriorating. He watched as relationships among the team, with several key customers, and with senior management took on a whole new flavor. And it wasn't pretty! Customers were complaining and a few had threatened to take their business elsewhere. Then there was the "management doesn't care about us" theme that became the water cooler chant. Many saw these moves as the latest example of technology replacing people. Some were even starting a pool, betting on how soon the next "early retirement" offer would be made.

Tom took these concerns to Gerald, senior vice president of the sales department. Gerald knew things were strained, but hadn't known just how bad it was and was uncertain what to do. As they talked, he could see all of the ways management had sent employees the wrong signals during this change initiative. No one had ever taken the time to communicate with them or address the impact and underlying fears, real or imagined, that these changes in job responsibilities were generating. Gerald knew he needed to rebuild trust with his team on his own and through Tom. He had to get buy-in from them about the online systems so they could see how their time could be better spent and generate the new possibilities management was hoping would happen as a result of the new technology.

Each of the questions below directly connects to the practices that build your change intelligence factor in the area of engagement.

- Examine the roles of Tom and then Gerald. What would be your self-discipline strategies in this situation?

- What enabling and disabling perceptions were both parties holding?

- How might this company reengage its sales people? What specific actions appear appropriate to you?

Application 2: Harness the Power of Conversation

> *A conversation is the natural process*
> *by which people live together,*
> *create together, and change together.*
> —*Margaret Wheatley*

We live in conversations. They create our reality because what we say either out loud or only inside our heads drives our actions. Unlike communication, which individually centers on the speaker's intentions, conversations embrace a "we" focus. They evoke clarity and seek out a solution that better coordinates future actions. Conversations are the fertile medium through which we engage one another and build relationships that give our lives meaning. We cultivate the space where new possibilities can take root as we develop our abilities to express our thoughts and feelings, share our concerns, our hopes, our fears, and our dreams. Take a moment to consider whether the conversations you hold are supporting the outcomes you really want to produce. And, if you want to bring something new into your life, if you want something to change, what conversation needs to happen to bring about the change you want to create?

All conversations—those you have and those you don't—have consequences. Notwithstanding the variety of electronic media in use today, holding effective conversations is becoming a lost art. People talk at one another rather than with one another. We push our agendas, often at the expense of making someone else appear wrong and us right. Our personal fears keep us from the richness of a new opportunity. Things get lost in translation. Alas, sometimes our conversations kill our possibilities before they even have a chance to see the light of day. Breakdowns occur. Frustration grows and relationships fracture. The new practices we have been learning about—exerting personal discipline, thinking things through, and taking effective actions—work in concert to ensure that your conversations produce the results you really want. Change intelligence enhances your ability to develop your conversational powers, which is paramount to your success, personally and professionally.

If the purpose of a conversation is to coordinate everyone's actions to create a desired future, then there are four questions to ask yourself before you begin your next conversation:

- What outcome do I want to generate?

- What language will best move the conversation forward helping me gain clarity about what my colleagues want and toward generating a mutually agreeable outcome?

- What mood/emotional field do I need to work from to best facilitate reaching this outcome?

- What body stance will support my efforts?

These questions may seem familiar by now—they are the essential questions of the L-E-B Model in action. Exploring your answers reveals the tone, tenor, physicality, and mood that will best serve you during any conversation. While it would be nice to assume that your colleagues will have asked and answered these same questions for themselves, there is no guarantee.

The three strategies that follow are sure to enhance your conversational competence. To start, I'll introduce you to different types of conversations that have different purposes and therefore lead to different outcomes. Your growing change intelligence helps you better match the type of conversation you hold to the situation, which will enhance the outcome for everyone. From there I'll introduce you to the power behind understanding speech act theory and connect the act of speaking to the equally, if not more important, act of listening. You can achieve amazing results when you simply shift the listening and speech actions you are using during conversations. Finally, we'll look at a few unique words and their impact on conversations.

Discovering the Intention in Conversations

Every conversation has a form; every conversation has a function or intention. The overarching purpose behind any conversation is to coordinate your actions with the actions of others in order to move more effectively together. Knowing from the start that different types of conversations support different outcomes means that you must employ your change intelligence skills and choose wisely.

To begin you may want to reflect on your current conversational skills. What is the message you want to send through your conversations? Which type of conversation will best send your message in a way that generates outcomes that move the process forward? How do you ensure that your conversation supports an ongoing, positive, and strong relationship with the people involved? How do different conversations affect your stress level? Which conversations are you more willing or less willing to conduct?

Refer back to the Dance of Effective Action Model in chapter 2 (Figure 2.6). All of the dispositions are available to you in the moments of your conversations. From center, step into the dance of the conversation. Move with the warrior spirit when you want to make your points and then shift to the lover, which is open and receptive to the thoughts of others. You might shift to the magician when you offer out of the box thinking and hear new ideas to consider. Or become the Rock of Gibraltar when the conversation warrants you keeping your head and remaining steady while everyone else appears to lose their footing. What action disposition do you usually adopt during challenging conversations? What about when you feel threatened? How might changing your disposition choice allow you to change the conversation you are able to hold and perhaps its results?

Here is an example to consider. You are rushing to an important meeting with a new customer when a co-worker stops you in the hall and blurts out details of a problem he is having with a customer. He is clearly agitated and defensive as he tells his side of the story. He wants your advice right then and there. Your mind is on your meeting, but you sense trouble brewing if you don't do something. The savior archetype living inside you wants to help. However, at this moment, and in this place, your effectiveness is compromised. Your focus is on the meeting where your warrior archetype is determined to win a new customer.

This situation has no single right answer. While the old you might have jumped right in, the new you, armed with your growing change intelligence skills, recognizes there are too many variables to consider in too narrow a time frame and you have too little of the information you need to be truly helpful. At this juncture, it is important simply to know that there are several different types of conversations that may prove fruitful to hold. Clearly, the one you choose will depend on different elements like time constraints, people involved, relationship status, and competing priorities. As you review Figure 3.5 below, consider which type of conversation you would choose to hold to handle this very common situation.

Figure 3.5 Types of Conversations

Category	Purpose	Defining Question	Description
Speculative Conversations	Conversations about Conversations	To accomplish our goals, what do we need to discuss, when, and how?	Establish time frame and subject of the conversation. Allow everyone to come prepared to participate fully. Emotions, mood, and body dispositions play a role.
	Conversations for Possibilities	What if	Clarify situation details and outcomes desired. Brainstorm and assess a full range of possible actions.
Action Conversations	Conversations for Action	What do we do next?	Use full range of requests, offers, and commitments to achieve desired goals. Clearly describe satisfaction and assessment standards.
	Conversations around Breakdowns	What happened? What now?	Acknowledge the breakdown and how it impacts the work and relationships. Decide next steps.
Community-Building Conversations	Orientation Conversations	Who are we?	Set context for the group. Connections develop as people embrace organizational success stories and share the meaning behind important events.
	Trust Conversations	Can I trust you? Can you trust me?	Build trusting relationships to support collective and independent actions. Openly address any and all issues that could potentially damage relationships.

Source: Adapted and used with permission from Newfield Network, Inc.

Coming to any conversation fully centered, where your capacity to take effective action is the greatest, increases your influence and leverage during the conversation. There are several ways to center yourself. Start with a scan of your L-E-B domains. Since emotion often precedes action, discerning your emotional field provides the most valuable information. Review Figure 3.6 and consider the power each emotion shown might have during the conversation. Which emotional field is in control? Your body is probably sending you signals to help answer the mood/emotion question. Centering yourself will give you more control of your actions, and you will be more able to counter any triggers that could otherwise pull you off course.

Figure 3.6 Emotions in Conversations

Emotions in Conversations

	Facts *"It is what it is"*	Possibilities *"What if..."*
Oppose what is	Resentment	Resignation Hopelessness
Accept what is *(no need to like it)*	At Peace Contentment Acceptance	Curiosity Enthusiasm Ambition

Source: Adapted with permission from Newfield Network, Inc.

Your ability to dance during the conversation also helps. Think salsa. Think cha-cha. Feel the pulse of the conversation unfolding before you. Consider when determined language will best serve the situation, when to be open and receptive to the thoughts and concerns of others, when to explore and play with possibilities like a magician, and when to ground yourself in strength. No two conversations are alike. Each one takes its own course. Remember always step back to center so that you can listen, receive what is being offered, and then take your next step.

> *The right conversation in the wrong mood*
> *is the wrong conversation.*
> *—Julio Olalla*

Using Speech Acts Skillfully

We all learn about the parts of speech in school—nouns, verbs, adjectives, to name just a few. Learning about the actions your speech evokes, however, is missing from most curriculums. First identified by James Austin (1973), speech act theory examines the building blocks of conversations. When we speak, we initiate action; we create new beginnings even as we end other situations and relationships.

According to Austin, there are five basic speech acts: assertions, declarations, requests, offers, and promises/commitments. Each one serves a specific purpose in a conversation. As you learn about speech acts and begin to more effectively use them during your conversations, you may find that you achieve your desired outcomes more easily.

Assertions. An assertion is a factual statement, easily verified by a witness or evidence. Assertions are true or false. *"Carl teaches math at Central High."* You can look at the faculty list and verify this assertion. *"My suit is navy blue."* is also easily verified as there is an agreed upon understanding of what navy blue looks like. Both statements are assertions.

Declarations. Statements that set the context for action and change reality are declarations. The person making the declaration must have the authority to make it. Four different types of declarations exist: beginning, ending, resolving, and assessing. Of the four, assessing is the one that causes people the most trouble and is in a league of its own. *"Emily is the new project manager."* is a beginning declaration. It starts something new that was not in existence prior to this declaration. On the opposite end, *"You are fired."* is an ending declaration. Ending declarations bring closure. What was is no longer. A simple *"Thank you for your hospitality."* is another form of ending declaration bringing closure to an evening with friends. A third type of declaration resolves issues. Again, having the appropriate authority is required. An example of a resolving declaration is *"The R&D budget will be cut, not the marketing budget."*

The fourth type of declaration, the one that is most problematic, is called an assessment. Assessments are neither true nor false. They are not facts. They are expressions of a person's opinion about something. Assessments can only be valid or invalid, and they require grounding, that is, information to support them. Assessments are based on past experience but made in present time. They frame future action. For example, you may have had a good experience with a vendor in the past. Now as you are evaluating companies to use on a current project, that past positive experience will ground your current opinion and lead to future actions with this company. By the same token, if the past experience was not good, that too will color the current situation. If new information about the past issue with the vendor is revealed, it could further change your assessment.

Too often assessments are said with such force or by someone in an authority position that they are held as assertions (facts). It is important to ground any assessment you make and listen carefully for grounding points when others are speaking. When you hear others making assessments, make sure you ask for their supporting data. Although you will not always be in a position to ask the person making the assessment for grounding data, challenging the assessment in your own mind and not blindly accepting it as fact is vital. For example, *"The report was done in a professional manner."* is an assessment. What does professional mean to this person? How does that compare with your interpretation of professional work?

Requests. When making requests, you are asking for something that you perceive is missing or needed in order to better coordinate future action. Requests may be formatted as questions, suggestions, propositions, orders (military, emergencies), demands, or invitations. Clearly, some formats work better than others. To be effective, requests need to be specific about what is needed or perceived as missing, the action warranted to fulfill the request, the conditions that must be met to satisfy the person making it, a time frame, and any other information necessary to fully understand what is needed.

Here are two examples of a common request. Note the different elements included in one and not the other. Which is stronger?

Can we meet tomorrow to talk about the presentation?

Kathy, I'd like to meet with you tomorrow at 2:00 p.m. to review our game plan for the sales presentation we are delivering together at the conference next week.

The person making the request must believe that the person on the receiving end has the appropriate skills and can be trusted to complete it. And most important, outside of emergency or military command situations, "no" must be a legitimate response to a request without fear or threat of retribution. I'll expand on the "no" response later in the chapter.

Offers. Recognizing a need and then volunteering your services are the basic framework for offers, which generally fall into two categories. The first category centers on your skills and talents. You know what your strengths are and what you can do well. You see a need, and make a relevant offer to help. Like requests, offers have criteria that frame them. You are specific about what you are offering, the time frame of the offer, and its boundaries. For example, you offer to design the new marketing materials for a local nonprofit encasing the offer with a one-month time frame and establishing the boundaries of the offer as a single brochure.

The second category of offers is you. Each of us is a unique person and therefore is an offer. Think about that for a moment. You are an offer in the world. You have gifts and talents to share. You can make a difference. I'll be expanding on this idea of you as an offer in the application about leading and serving. For the moment, just let this idea stew in your mind. Let it begin to tickle your curiosity about you as an offer. You may want to ask your manager or colleagues what they consider your most powerful contribution at work. Their responses may surprise you and open a new area of self-awareness exploration for you. Try it!

Commitments. Making a commitment to do a particular action is the last piece of the request/offer cycle and the final speech act. When you make a request or offer to someone, you present them with a choice. That person can then respond with a yes or a no. Often there will be ways to negotiate the terms of a request or an offer. Eventually decision time arrives and the dance ends in some variation of yes or no. And again, outside of military or emergency situations, both answers must be available. If both responses are not acceptable, you are denying someone dignity and may find yourself lied to and disappointed. Think about it. If your ego is so fragile that it cannot accept no as a viable answer, what does it say about you? Fulfilling your commitments is the glue that holds everything together and builds your reputation in the world. Relationships are made and lost on the basis of promises kept and promises broken.

In addition to the five basic speech acts, the other key component in skillful conversations is listening. Listening is fast becoming a lost art, much to the detriment of effective communication. It is transparent until something happens to indicate that what was said was not fully heard. When you deconstruct listening's components, you find two discrete actions: hearing and interpretation. Because each speech act element has a clear framework, you can better discern how you are listening:

- What are you listening for—facts, opinions, points to challenge?
- Is your listening being affected by who is speaking?
- Are you a better listener when you agree with what is being said?
- What happens to your listening when you disagree?
- Are you really listening or are you busy figuring out how you plan to counter what is being said?
- What happens to your listening when what is being said is outside your frame of reference?

Practicing active listening requires that you become aware of the answers you might give to the questions above. Awareness of the factors that impact how you listen enables you to exert the discipline you need to keep your attention where it belongs—on the speaker and what is being said. Your developing introspection skills allow you to assess how your personal biases and perceptions are affecting your listening. What filters are in place, and how are these filters coloring your interpretations? Listening also requires you to observe how the speaker is being present. What emotions may be evident? What body disposition is in control? What is the tone and texture of the language? As you grow as a listener, your subsequent actions connect with people, show real care and concern, and offer responses that are relevant to the situation at hand and insightful.

Introducing speech acts to your colleagues is a great way to invent a commitment culture. These tools facilitate strong relationships, strong organizations, strong communities, and strong families. They provide the structure that makes accepting accountability easier. Speech acts change the conversations from blame and struggle to possibilities and opportunities. Figure 3.7 provides a visual image for how an initial request conversation leads to commitment, performance, delivery, and feedback when speech acts are embedded into the process.

Figure 3.7 Accountability Wheel

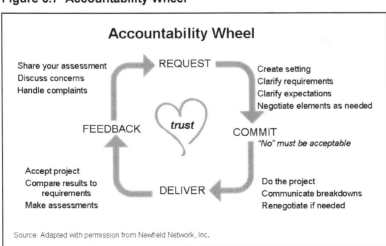

Source: Adapted with permission from Newfield Network, Inc.

Choosing Your Words Wisely

Conversations are word flows between participants. The primary question to ask yourself is what seeds do you water with your words? The words you choose and the emotional field within which they are delivered hold the key to the outcomes you generate. They either move the conversation forward or put it into a defensive mode. There are words that bring people together as surely as there are "fighting words"—words that pull us apart. Take a moment to think about how your word choices might be helping or hindering any of your current efforts to get what you want. When we believe that our conversations have the ability to yield more powerful results, we begin to approach each one with a newfound respect for the act itself.

Choosing more effective words that better represent both openness to others and your own opinion about how to move forward takes some learning. Here are a few easy changes that produce huge payoffs.

- *Shoulda–Coulda–Woulda.* I once heard "should" described as a word that was invented to make our lives miserable. Along with its friends, "coulda" and "woulda," it is weighed down with assessments of right and wrong and emotions like guilt. These words are result of the story we tell ourselves about an experience we have had or one that presents itself for our consideration. I should have done "x." Or I should do "y." There is no "should," no "could," and, really, no "would." There is only a choice before you. Behind any of these words is a request that we need to make of ourselves or to someone else. Replace your "should," "could," and "would" with more assertive language. Use "will" instead. "I will" and then do it. Or "I will not" and don't. Then let go of the emotion as it is wasted energy.

- *"And" not "But."* "But" stops the forward motion of a conversation in its tracks. When someone hears a "but" the person's defenses go on high alert. What comes after the "but" often escalates a situation and highlights differences. If you are the listener, a better strategy is to validate what the other person said, showing that you actually were listening before you offer a competing idea. If you are the speaker, work to replace the "but" with "and." You'll have to choose different words to use once "and" is in charge of the second portion of any sentence. Watch what happens. The power of this small shift from adversary to collaborator is tremendous.

- *"No."* At just two little letters, the word "no" is deceptively powerful. The emotional reaction to hearing "no" or wanting to say "no" overwhelms too many people. Many are afraid of using the word and become victims of situations that quickly move out of their control. And while most people consider "no" in negative terms, allowing it into your life is the only way to legitimize your conversations and honor yourself. When you reposition it as just another word, like apple, box, dog, it opens opportunities for everyone concerned. It dignifies the issue of the conversation, repositioning it outside of you personally. Think about the times you have said "yes" but wanted to say "no." What was missing for you that trapped you in an untenable situation where you had to lie? "No" rarely means never. It just means that right now I can't do "x." When joined with "and" these words become a dynamic duo. "No, I can't do "x" and ...." You could then offer options, a timing difference, any number of conditions under which the "no" can shift to "yes."

- *"How"* or *"What,"* not *"Why."* Learning how to ask powerful questions of yourself and others is a skill worthy of your time and attention. Your goal is always the same—to open the space for discovery. Think of questioning as peeling an onion. The thin outer layer is papery, while layers toward the core are thicker. During the questioning process, you peel back the event itself, layer by layer, working to expose the innermost core, what's real and true. You immerse yourself in questions, evoking more expansive inquiry of what happened unfettered by shades of meaning or ego-driven story elements. You observe the what and how of things, allowing these elements to percolate before probing deeper into why. Questioning interpretations opens exploration and reveals areas ripe for change.

- *"Thank You" and "You're Welcome."* These two powerful phrases used together bring closure to many situations and let people know they are appreciated. Often the words "thanks" and "thank you" get said automatically—they have become almost throw-away expressions. Adding the "you're welcome" closes the appreciation loop. After all, these two phrases are among the very first learned when learning a new language. Why should they be any less important in our first language?

As you take more time to consider your words, and incorporate language that truly promotes the outcomes you seek, interesting developments may occur. When you mean what you say and actually say what you mean, generating results more in line with your goals will become easier. Higher-order language skills cultivate a cooperative spirit, bringing people together in powerful ways. Your increased skill with language is the outcome of your developing change intelligence.

> *You were born with the creative power*
> *of the universe at the tip of your tongue.*
> *—Neale Donald Walsch, in*
> Conversations with God

Insights for Action

Conversations are your doorway to a world of opportunity because they directly impact your relationships. Harnessing the power inherent in conversations to produce the results you really want can be very challenging, especially when your emotions are triggered. It is in conversations that old habits die hard. Accept that it's not about what happens to you; it's about what you do. Yes, in this context, it is all about you.

My coaching here asks that you see improving your conversational prowess as a two-step process. First, from your reading, you are learning how to interpret what happens to you from multiple perspectives thus empowering you to see events beyond the surface. Second, you are challenged you to take the high road. Hold your dignity intact and use language that expresses your concerns in a non-threatening manner. You know you have options using the Dance of Effective Actions. Center yourself and then choose language that allows you to respond to what is happening in ways that show you are in charge. Being in charge does not equate to blaming or banging heads or extracting your pound of flesh. Being in charge means being generous with your comments, being thoughtful and caring. These two steps showcase the essence of change intelligence.

What you will begin to notice as you enter into more powerful conversations is that your world changes because your conversations are changing. Incorporating new tools and techniques gives you the confidence to engage in high-stakes conversations rather than run from them. Keep poking the boundaries of your comfort zone to uncover new actions that may better support your desired outcomes. Realize that making even one small change can have huge ramifications. Your influence grows as others see you as someone who can self-manage the emotional components of conversations, forgoing ego for outcome. These may seem like small changes at first. What you will notice is that they produce significant results.

ACTIVITY: Requests and Offers

Practice making effective requests and offers by using the two worksheets presented here. Think about something you want or need. Now fill in the elements of your request/offer to make sure it is complete and the person on the receiving end will have all the details he or she needs to be able to respond.

Activity: Requests and Offers

Requests Worksheet (Asking for What I Need)
What is the problem/issue/situation?
What emotions do I need to be mindful of to ensure that my request can be heard?
What are the specifics that I see as missing?
What are the requirements and criteria that fulfill the need?
If not me, who is the best person to do the work?
What is the time frame? Is it negotiable? If yes, to what extent?
What do I or others helping me need to know about the situation in order to do a good job?
What standard will I use to assess the work as acceptable?

Now let's repeat the same process focusing on making an offer. Look around you. I am confident that you will find many opportunities to stand up and make an offer.

Offers Worksheet (How I Can Help)
What specific need do I see where I have a skill that can help?
What emotions do I need to be mindful of to ensure that my offer can be heard?
What are the specifics I see as missing?
What are the identifiable requirements I see to frame my offer?
Who is the best person to make my offer to?
What is the time frame within which I can complete my offer? Is it negotiable? If yes, to what extent?
What questions do I need to ask to ensure my offer fulfills the need?
What standard will I use to assess my work as acceptable?

Application 3: Embrace the Possibility of Conflict

Conflicts and obstacles teach us lessons
we refuse to learn in an easier way.
—I Ching

Conflict is the recognition of a gap between what exists and what we want to exist. It is neither good nor bad in and of itself. When breakdowns occur, when differences emerge, the emotions triggered can generate exciting results—sometimes positive, sometimes negative. If these energies are targeted at the breakdown, conflict's friction has the potential to become constructive, igniting everyone's creative juices about how to make the situation better.

Unfortunately, because conflict makes many people feel uncomfortable and out of control, the energies are often directed at either ignoring the conflict or blaming or attacking the people involved. Fed by fears, conflict breeds in unspoken expectations, unfulfilled promises and commitments, or outright disagreements. Often conflicts are triggered when we become aware of our own deficiencies and refuse to learn new strategies to address them. We can get stuck—and stuck is often predicated on a past that, while no longer relevant, continues to hold us hostage to its power. The faster you recognize your "stuckness" the better. Rather than staying stuck, wallowing in your personal breakdown, use introspection to honestly explore what got you into this mess. As should be becoming clear by now, the process of introspection plays a critical role in all aspects of developing your change intelligence. Here are a few thought-provoking questions to help guide your conflict reflection session:

- What actions do you take when conflict comes a calling?

- What results are these actions producing?

- Are they the results you want?

- What do you need to learn about yourself in order to make conflict your ally?

Once you have a better understanding of yourself and the situation, you can then shift your focus and consider strategies to get you unstuck. Harnessing your change intelligence in these situations allows you to embrace conflict as a beneficial energy that can focus your thoughts on seeking solutions, drive positive outcomes, and lead to sustainable change.

Because your goal is to increase your ability to change your own behaviors in ways that best serve your goals and produce better results, reviewing the labels assigned to popular conflict strategies and styles might be a helpful place to start. Most strategies to deal with conflict aim at two (sometimes competing) objectives: attaining goals and maintaining relationships. Figure 3.8 is a compilation of conflict styles and strategies. Each style purports to accomplish one or both of these objectives to a greater or lesser extent. For example, forcing might be very effective in attaining goals but ineffective at maintaining relationships; conversely, appeasing would score high on the relationship scale but low on the goals scale. Cooperating and collaborating as strategies are effective at both resolving problems (attaining what you want) and maintaining strong relationships in the process. As you review the figure below, think about which style labels fit your actions and whether your actions are situation dependent.

Figure 3.8 Conflict Styles and Strategies

Style/Strategy	Description
Forcing Competing Overpowering Fighting	You want your needs met at all costs, so you use a very aggressive and overpowering style. The cliché, "it's my way or the highway" fits here, as does "I win, you lose."
Accommodating Appeasement Smoothing Yielding	You relinquish your needs and goals for the sake of others. Your need to be liked and included takes precedence over getting your other needs met.
Avoiding Withdrawing	You work to remove yourself from conflict situations. Feelings of helplessness overpower you and you shut down. Everyone loses here because the conflict issue does not go away. It is always present below the surface, tainting the relationships and success of the members. Remember no decision is still a decision.
Compromising Conciliating	You are willing to give up some part of what you want and expect others to do likewise. It's the "win some–lose some" approach. That way, no one gets all of what they want, and the relationships are maintained at what is perceived as an acceptable level.
Cooperating Collaborating	Seeking the higher win, this style focuses everyone's energies on the problem, seeking to both solve it and maintain strong relationships in the process.

The problem with all of these strategies, however, is that they are missing an important element—what is going on inside you. Your thoughts, and the emotions they trigger, have a huge impact on your behavior and outcomes. Take compromise as an example. When you compromise, you are giving up a portion of what you want, and you expect the other person to do the same thing. But what if you assess that what you are giving up is more valuable than what the other person has agreed to relinquish? What if you judge your solution as better? What if this is the umpteenth time this week that you have been forced to compromise? These thoughts and feelings can play Ping-Pong in your brain even as you agree to compromise, and they don't necessarily disappear when you shake hands. They certainly don't magically disappear when you get to work. So while the external conflict is resolved, the internal conflict (the emotions it engenders) can remain, simmering just below the surface. And if you feel cheated or taken advantage of, anger and resentment can fester and grow. Each compromise has the potential to chip away at your relationships and diminish your effectiveness.

Those who are defensive do not understand.
Those who understand have nothing to defend.
—Lao Tzu

Turning Conflict into an Opportunity Generator

So if the usual strategies to deal with conflict are inadequate, how can you learn to channel conflict's energy into productive actions that both produce the results you want and strengthen important relationships? How can you learn to reposition conflict from negative and disruptive to generative and productive and open wide the doorway to creative thinking, collaboration, and truly masterful levels of problem solving?

The seeds to assist you in making the disruptive-to-generative shift are the major themes we have already been learning about—exerting personal discipline, growing your observer and introspection capabilities to inform your judgment, and then choosing more effective actions. This is the core of developing greater change intelligence and learning to dance with change. As you can see, your own thoughts and actions again play a starring role. How to actually operationalize this process is the learning nugget.

Breakdowns (conflict) happen to everyone. You are going along and then something happens that stops you cold. Two critical questions emerge and directly point to your opportunity during any breakdown. The first is the "now what" question. *What do I need to do now to handle what has happened so that I can get back on track and resume my course of action?* In most instances you know what to do. It can be something easy to fix (like the copier needing paper) or something more intense (like arriving at the airport to find your flight canceled). Putting more paper in the copier resolves the issue. Using an app on your iPad or Smartphone or talking to a customer service representative at the airport to reschedule your flight may not be as easy to do, but you know these are the steps you need to take.

The second question is a bit more complex, and for our learning purposes, it reigns supreme: *How do I need to do it?* Change intelligence is all about the "how." What you do next, in the heat of this moment, reveals a lot about you. Filling the copier is a no brainer, but what about talking to the swamped customer service representative? Your ability to handle what comes next in an emotionally intelligent way is critical to your ongoing success. Are you the nice guy or the jerk? And depending on your mental and emotional state, either is a possibility. While you can have an adult hissy fit (and it might feel good to explode), its results won't bring you closer to your short- or long-term goals.

Exerting personal discipline is vital when the necessity to change your plans is thrust upon you. Quickly assessing where your L-E-B domains are and whether separation is imminent is a good place to start. Consider the following list of process-based questions to guide your introspection. Notice that the speech acts discussed earlier play an important role in diagnosing the full scope of the issue. Your answers will give you the clues you need to take effective action in any conflict situation.

- What is the issue?

- How did I get myself into this mess (ego, jealousy, pride, envy, greed, failure to act) or does the cause lie elsewhere?

- What assessments am I holding that are relevant to this conflict?

- How have I verified the validity of these assessments?

- What outcome do I really want?

- What do I need to do to get what I want?

Let's apply these questions to another example. Read the story below and then consider the full scope of Manny's predicament. You are Manny's mentor. How might you help him admit that he has a breakdown to address, that he needs to sort through and analyze the underlying issues creating his situation, and that he must then identify new actions to produce different results?

> *Manny is the night shift help-desk agent at a large customer call center. The last six months have been tough. He resents working nights, but it was the only job he could get in a tight economy with a two-year degree from the local community college. He wants to be out gallivanting with his friends but needs the job to support a family he had not planned on having at this point in his life. His wife is a nurse at the health care clinic around the corner. It is a good job, but she comes home emotionally drained and after taking care of the baby, she has little reserve energy to listen to Manny's complaints. As a result, Manny has developed an attitude. At work, his responses to help requests have turned into rude rants that offend clients. He is short tempered with co-workers who would occasionally seek his opinion. Within a short time, the IT manager was overwhelmed with complaints and threats to cancel contracts. He pulled the call center tapes from the previous week and noted Manny's callous treatment of clients. He has asked Manny to come in early tonight to have a talk. The call from his boss has shaken Manny. He fears he will be fired from his job. Manny has called you because he respects your opinion and knows that he needs help before the meeting with his boss tonight.*

- *What is the issue?* Manny has several issues to deal with right now. A new family, a basic skill level that limits his opportunities, and a job he doesn't respect. Can you think of other issues confronting Manny?

- *How did Manny get himself in this mess?* Manny's short-term thinking, immaturity, and need for immediate gratification overtook his thinking. He clearly did not appreciate the long-term consequences of his actions, resulting in family responsibilities, a low-level job, and less time to party with friends.

- *What assessments is Manny holding and how has he validated them?* Manny probably holds assessments about his capabilities. Challenging these assessments one by one will enable Manny to separate those that are valid and grounded in facts from those that are no longer valid. As he examines his assessments, he can reveal new truths to himself about what is possible going forward.

- *What outcome does Manny really want?* Here is where conflict as opportunity generator shows up. Asking Manny to describe the life he wants to be living and how he envisions his future is important. His responses will help him identify and prioritize future actions and align them with what he really wants. The challenge will be to help him better define the life he wants to be living long term.

- *What does he need to do to get what he wants?* Depending on how Manny answers the previous question, action options will surface. If he wants to keep his job, he will have to reestablish trust with his boss.

As you can appreciate from the example above, it is important to peel back the layers of excuses and rationalization to get at the core issues motivating behavior. Using these questions to explore conflict situations more thoroughly is generative and yields opportunities where once there were only dead ends. The ultimate goal is to better coordinate the actions of all parties specifically targeted at achieving the agreed-upon goals. Embracing change intelligence gives you a strategic advantage. Because you are learning how to change your own behaviors first, you can shift the dynamic to the classic "win-win" more easily. Others see you as someone who can lead because you are taking responsibility for your own actions. Your power to influence outcomes grows as you exhibit higher levels of relationship building.

Conflict is a strange bedfellow. One interesting point you may notice is that the conflict situations people find themselves in appear eerily similar. The people may change, but the details of the conflict have a certain sameness; often centering on core issues such as fears, out-of-control anger, resentments, or trust/confidence issues. The critical truism here is that you are the key player at the root of every conflict that you find yourself in. When you learn the underlying lesson that the conflict is trying to teach you, you can apply change intelligence practices to develop a more empowering narrative about yourself, which allows you to take more effective actions. The underlying elements of this particular conflict will diminish as new conflicts show up. All are designed to help you grow and transform yourself in ways that support living up to your full potential—delivering on the promise of extra-ordinary.

> *It is a painful thing to look at your own trouble*
> *and know that you yourself,*
> *and no one else, has made it.*
> *—Sophocles*

Building Prudent Trust

Trust is the foundation of all human interactions, and it plays a critical role during conflicts. Because trust roots itself in the emotional domain, and the emotional domain powers your performance, the more you trust yourself and others, the stronger your performance becomes. When trust is low or missing, your productivity suffers. For some people, extending trust is as natural as breathing. For others, trust must be earned as a result of observable actions. The bottom line here is that without trust, there can be no commitment. Without commitments, getting things done with and through others proves extremely difficult, and people and projects suffer.

Julio Olalla (2001) defines trust as the "emotions that go around the way we deal with each other when we make promises to one another." And the size or magnitude of these promises makes no difference. The big promises of life—"until death do us part" or "I'll love you forever"—are certainly important and can cause us to suffer if they are broken. The day-to-day commitments and promises we make to one another that undergird the majority of our relationships are equally important to the health of our relationships. I'm talking about the "I'll get the report to you by noon" or "I'll call you back in five minutes," or even "I'll pick up the milk on my way home" kind of statements that litter our days. As you keep—or don't keep—your commitments, co-workers and others in your life make an assessment about your trustworthiness. Were you being sincere? Do you have the skills to do what you said? Are you reliable? Will you do what it takes to complete the commitment?

At times we break trust and need to mend the breach. Once broken, reestablishing trust will require a concerted effort on your part. The starting point is a heartfelt apology, followed up by your willingness to fix your mistakes and live up to your promises day by day. It is important to note, however, that once you have owned your part, the decision to trust you again is out of your hands.

Trusting people carries with it the risk of disappointment, which is precisely where conflict shows up. While the emotion behind disappointment stops many people from trusting others, a better strategy is to insert the word *prudent* before trust. Prudent trust makes full use of grounded assessments. It presents the opportunity for a conversation should someone expect your trust and not deserve it in your opinion. They can't change and remedy what they do not fully understand. Your ability to speak about the breach of trust, your assessment of the factors behind your unwillingness to extend trust, and the conditions under which you will offer another trust opportunity create only the possibility, not the guarantee, of continuing the relationship. The other person can decline to change or falsely promise to change and do nothing. When this happens, the conflict can grow until the breakdown becomes overwhelming and the relationship fractures. At this point the people can each go their own way. Unfortunately, in some work situations people feel trapped and they try to continue to work together, accepting that there is no trust.

Because trust is formed as a result of the promises and commitments we keep and don't keep, it can be illuminating to examine three different types of promises (Figure 3.9). Think about how each type of promise shows up in your own daily interactions.

Figure 3.9 Three Types of Promises

Type of Promise	Distinction
Healthy	A promise we can and will keep.
Shallow	A promise made with the best of intentions. You have unshared information and awareness that a condition already exists that may prevent you from keeping it.
Criminal	A promise made with no intention to keep it, usually labeled a lie.
Source: Used with permission from Newfield Network, Inc.	

Consider, for example, the breach of trust one of my clients recently experienced. Due to a number of factors, his company was again playing with employees' pay increases. Not only were the performance evaluations not delivered within the time frame stipulated by senior management, no communication had been generated to inform employees about the delay or reasons behind it. The question my client struggled with was both pointed and poignant: How can he, as a department manager, be trusted when his hands were tied about this most fundamental workplace issue, pay? He knew employees were creating their own stories around why the raises were delayed and that those stories would not be conducive to optimal performance. The company has clearly broken a promise to its employees. The company's failure to communicate about the delay and the reason behind it exacerbated the trust breach.

Can you identify the types of promises in this example? My client clearly understood how important it is to his role as an effective manager to be trusted and seen as someone who makes (and keeps) healthy promises. Through no fault of his own, however, he was forced into being an unwilling broker of a shallow promise, and the effects of these broken promises are equally clear to him. His company, by breaking its promise to its employees, is at best dealing in shallow promises and at worst criminal ones.

Growing your change intelligence in this one area will significantly benefit your relationships and your well-being. Consider all of your relationships and various situations you experience. What you are looking for are any patterns of behavior that emerge from the promises you experience and where these show up. For example, are there people with whom you only make healthy promises? Can you isolate relationships and situations where your promises sit on shaky ground, where there is a "but" hiding in the weeds? Finally, can you think of people and situations where you do not have the inner courage to be truthful and therefore make promises you know full well that you have no intention of keeping?

The caveat, of course, is that there are times when our commitments must be renegotiated. As we have discussed, breakdowns happen. They are a fact of life. What you do when a breakdown occurs and the timing of your actions speaks volumes about how you respect the relationship, and ultimately how you respect yourself. Many people wait until the very last minute before admitting they can't deliver. The person on the receiving end must then hustle and renegotiate any promise he or she made that relied on your deliverable.

There is a better way, one that allows everyone involved to better coordinate actions and keep relationships strong. Refer back to the Accountability Wheel in Figure 3.7. During the performance phase, breakdowns must be acknowledged and the promise renegotiated. The longer you wait, the closer you get to the agreed-upon delivery deadline, the greater the possibility of tainting trust and damaging the relationship.

Insights for Action

Developing effective conflict resolution skills is a key component of change intelligence. Repositioning conflicts as opportunities to solve problems can inject fresh energy into your life and organization. You play a starring role in all of your conflicts: something that you are doing, have done, are not doing, or have not done has contributed to your current state of affairs. Your actions (past and present) beget your outcomes, and there is no escape. There may be new players, a new job, a new relationship, a new location, but the root problem remains the same until you deal with it. And that root problem always goes to core personal issues, your ability to develop your humanness through your thoughts, your words, and your deeds.

Trust is foundational in dealing with conflict situations; it is critical, therefore, to take the time and energy to create, grow, maintain, and rebuild trust to improve your results. Positive, constructive conflict asks questions and explores possibilities to support expansive inquiry. The emotions expressed here are inventive, stimulating, and enthusiastic. When you and your peers or employees share different points of view in constructive ways, amazing ideas emerge that can lead to new products, services, and results. When done with integrity, your efforts will generate transparent and powerful returns for you.

ACTIVITY: Constructive Conflict

Think about a current conflict situation. Use the conflict strategy worksheet that follows to diagram the conflict's story. Notice your language. Identify the emotional energy being triggered by unfolding events. Remember that in any conflict, very familiar negative emotions emerge: anger, fear, guilt, dread, jealousy, frustration, anxiety, pride, arrogance, envy, pessimism, resignation, and resentment. Monitor your body's tension. Each domain of the L-E-B Model offers you a different perspective on how you are experiencing a conflict.

Try to discern how you arrived in the conflict situation and the variables that are holding power over you. Identify how your actions, words, or attitude contribute to differences that emerge to cause the conflict. Think about the situation from the other person's perspective. Are you using language or exhibiting attitude or emotions that appear to be triggers for others? Acknowledge these differences and work to separate them from the facts of the situation. Accept accountability and acknowledge your role in the conflict. From here, you can generate solutions that the others may be able to hear, consider, and accept.

Tap into the wisdom of questions. Self-discipline and introspection play an important role now. Ask yourself tough questions like the ones that appear below. Take the time to allow various levels of answers to percolate and emerge. Easy answers show up first. Be still. The more important answers take time to work their way into your consciousness. Seek to isolate the core personal growth opportunity that is being tested by the conflict. As noted author Richard Bach once wrote, "There is no such thing as a problem without a gift for you in its hands." So far, so good. What will really blow your mind is what he says next: "You seek problems because you need their gifts."

Conflict Strategy Worksheet

What is the issue?

Who is involved?

What is motivating me at the moment? How did I get myself into this mess? What fear or loss (real or perceived) is generating the conflict?

What do I perceive to be the position(s) of the other people involved?

What is my assessment of the relationships I have with this person/these people?

What emotions have been triggered? What am I feeling? Where are these feelings coming from?

What is my body communicating to me and to others?

What am I speaking out loud? What am I thinking and not saying?

Was there a real commitment made or am I assuming a commitment that the other person really did not make?

ACTIVITY: Constructive Conflict / Worksheet

What assessments (opinions) are here that I may be holding as assertions (facts)?

What words describe how I am acting in this conflict?

What outcome do I want regarding the issue?

What outcome do I want from the relationship?

How can I look at this differently to see new perspectives and options for resolution?

In what ways has this same issue shown up in previous conflicts?

What do I need to learn now that will get me through this conflict and have it not reappear?

What skills do I need to learn to be able to resolve this situation?

What actions can I take that will move me closer to acceptable outcomes for all involved?

1.

2.

3.

CASE STUDY

Ted recently participated in a three-day sales training session. He found himself disturbed by the language the trainer, Jim, was using to describe the company's customers. He kept calling them "marks" and berating their intelligence. For Ted, Jim's words showed a total lack of appreciation for the very people who kept them both employed. His respect for Jim was fading fast as Jim's demeaning comments continued.

When Ted returned for the third day of training, something had changed. As Jim started to speak he clearly caught himself as he was about to again belittle the customers. Ted could visibly see him choke back the disparaging remarks and replace them with words holding more positive regard. Later on, during a break, as Ted and a few other participants were having a discussion about some of the new sales tools being presented, Jim made eye contact with Ted and off-handedly called him a "spy."

During the drive home, Ted thought about the incident. He knew other participants shared similar sentiments about Jim's negativity from discussions during a break on the very first day. He wondered if any of them had spoken to Jim. Ted knew he had also mentioned the incident to his manager, Carl. He could not help but wonder if his words had gone full circle and brought about the change, especially in light of the "spy" comment.

Ted was concerned about his own standing in the company. When he got home, he sent an email to Carl and specifically asked if he had mentioned their conversation about Jim to anyone else. Within an hour Carl called him to say that he had been concerned and had spoken with his own manager about how to proceed. This discussion did in fact lead to action taken by management that resulted in Jim's effort to use more positive language on day three of the training. Carl wanted Ted to know about the conversation so that their relationship would remain on solid ground. He wanted to assure Ted that his concerns were heard and respected. Finally, Carl wanted to rebuild any lost trust so that Ted would continue to be an engaged member of the team and continue to express concerns.

This case represents several different conflicts. Each character has something to gain as well as something to lose. Your challenge:

- If you were Ted, how would you have handled this situation with Jim?

- If you were Carl, how would you have handled this situation with Ted and Jim?

- And, what about Jim? What would you do about Jim?

Application 4: Lead and Serve: The Promise of Extra-Ordinary Fulfilled

Effective leaders put words to the formless longings and deeply felt needs of others.
—Warren Bennis

There has been so much written about leadership one would think the topic fully covered. And yet, looking around, we see very few people who can describe a context for a desired future, generate the emotional energy to capture the commitment of others, and embody actions aligned with their vision that followers can witness and embrace. Yes, there are many people with fancy titles in jobs that designate them as the person in charge, the person with the power to tell people what to do, to make things happen. And yet, all around the world we see economies stagnating, financial problems crippling once-thriving nations, and people in need without the means and methods to address those needs. These supposed leaders talk at one another rather than with one another. They often cause more problems than they solve. Despite the power they hold, they still appear impotent. And power can be seductive. It places forces like manipulation and coercion at their disposal—neither of which proves sustainable when it comes to authentically engaging people to bring their creativity and talents to bear to solve real problems in the service of others. Clearly, something is missing.

Everything in the book to this point has been in preparation for this chapter. It has been about understanding how you can develop your change intelligence skills to not just survive the constant flux and change in your life and workplace but to thrive in it, to become the master of your destiny. It has been about knowing yourself and getting your internal house in order. It has been about learning to control your actions, to think through issues in productive ways, and then find the courage to take effective action. The models, discussions, and activities shared here are all designed for one purpose—to shift your self-orientation and forever change the context within which you operate. Becoming more self-aware allows you to appreciate yourself differently. You stop identifying with a past that is no longer relevant. You develop an identity more aligned to the person you are now and who you want to become. Your introspective practice brings to light multiple interpretations of events. Armed with varied perspectives, fresh insights emerge and breed more response possibilities. And all of this happens because you change the context—because you learn to trust your change intelligence.

Now that you are well on your way in this journey, there is a further step toward mastering the promise of extra-ordinary—leading and serving others. I would like to enable you to see yourself as someone who can contribute in ways you may have not thought possible. You are a gift to the world. Whoa! Remember when I first made this declaration in the conversational power application? I asked you to not dismiss it immediately, to simply let it stew a bit, to let it permeate your pores. While this idea may sound too new age for you to embrace, consider that leading and serving others, perceiving a need and working to meet it, is how you make a difference in the world. Seeing yourself as a contributor, someone whose efforts can make a difference in the lives of others, is empowering.

And in my mind, this is the best definition of leadership: seeing a need and willingly stepping up to the challenge of addressing it. An authentic leader is someone who inspires others, harnessing his or her own courage while enlisting the courage and commitment of others to pursue a different future for themselves and their communities. Authentic leadership expresses the highest form of service to others.

The beauty of my definition of leadership with service to others at its core is its universal application. Everyone can find opportunities to serve and through their efforts begin to see new possibilities for themselves. In this context, it is through leading that you experience your own growth and begin to truly master the promise of extra-ordinary.

The models, practices, and applications we have been exploring together to enhance our change intelligence offer a roadmap for leadership growth as well. You'll find that many of the questions remain the same. The difference here is that your personal goal is to practice authentic leadership, striving to serve others through your public actions. Your focus and energies are targeted outside of yourself, and this is only possible because you have already done the internal hard work. You stand on firm ground, confident, strong. Your external actions exhibit authenticity that attracts others, regardless of whether they are your colleagues, your customers, or your community. In your mind, the questions are clear: *"What do you need? How can I help?"*

The challenge of leadership is to be strong, but not rude;
be kind, but not weak; be bold, but not bully; be thoughtful, but not
lazy; be humble, but not timid; be proud, but not arrogant; have
humor, but without folly.
—Jim Rohn

Owning the Learning Piece

I think we can all agree that there are a few people who naturally match my description of an authentic leader. They inherently know who they are and are comfortable in their own skin. They know how to be, even when they may not know specifically what to do. Authentic leadership and strong change intelligence seem to be part of their DNA.

I believe strongly that this way of being can be developed through learning. You can learn how to develop the type of authenticity that inspires others to follow. The change intelligence practices we have been discussing to this point have laid the groundwork for your actions.

Change intelligence is the critical factor in how leaders respond in learning situations. Learning is synonymous with change. What do you need to learn in order to change? What new behaviors do you need to practice to rewire your consciousness to thrive regardless of the specifics of a given situation?

In this essential link between learning and authentic leadership, there are five important lessons to bear in mind: 1) authentic leaders learn (simple, but with profound implications); 2) exemplary leaders are exemplary followers first; 3) authentic leaders inspire; 4) authentic leaders bounce (that is, they are flexible and resilient); and 5) authentic leaders practice leading.

Leaders Learn*.* Your first important learning is that the act of learning is your friend. Leaders don't know everything. What they do know is how to learn. Through learning what you don't know and how to see through the clutter, your ability to lead reveals itself. Not knowing stops so many people from achieving because of the stigma attached to admitting that they don't have the answers. Rather than allowing the fear of not knowing to freeze you in your tracks, accept your vulnerability and embrace it courageously. Answers exist. You need only look outside of yourself for them.

Leaders Follow. Another important learning focuses on your ability to learn how to be an exemplary follower. Leadership and followership are complementary roles. No one leads all the time, and everyone is accountable to someone. Following is not a passive activity. Moreover, how you show up when it is time to perform as a follower speaks volumes about how you lead. The behaviors of exemplary followers, when examined more deeply, are the same behaviors authentic leaders embrace. For example, exemplary followers share their best ideas willingly with the project's goals in mind. Just like leaders. Followers take full responsibility for their own actions in support of the project's success. Just like leaders. Followers use appropriate conversational tools, choosing language that moves the work forward. Just like leaders. Followers mind their attitudes, radiating a willingness to accept someone other than themselves in the leader position.

Leaders Inspire. A third important learning requires leaders to inspire and align people around a vision of what is possible. From here they galvanize their intrinsic energies to produce actions that deliver on that vision. Yes, here is the context point again. Leadership is not about you—it's about them. Paint a picture of a desired future that people can support and that they want. Then shepherd their process. The leader's role has many facets—teacher, coach, mentor, and cheerleader. Supporting others as they try out new behaviors can be transformative. It speaks to a shared accountability of being humans together and goes well beyond hiring and retaining talented people. The challenge is deeper and richer. Inspiring people beyond their own self-perceived limitations opens up a world of possibility for them. Show them a different roadmap, a fresh landscape of how their lives can unfold, how they can contribute. Then do everything in your power to support their learning so that they can achieve the vision. And helping others achieve their goals and dreams is inspiring. That is true leadership.

Leaders Bounce. Learning how to bounce is important. What I am really talking about here is resilience. In the Dance of Change Model, this is the magician archetype at its best. We all know that things don't always go the way we want them to go. Breakdowns happen all the time. We know that bad things happen to good people. We know that there is evil in the world. You can get caught up in this—or you can bounce. Authentic leaders bounce—and bounce high. Because they are grounded in their values, they have learned fortitude, and their confidence in their own abilities is strong. Learn how to muster your resilience; resist seeing yourself as a victim of forces beyond your control. Getting up when knocked down requires practice. As you get better recovering your footing, you will find yourself increasing your challenges, raising your own bar on the projects that you undertake.

Leaders Practice. To become an effective leader you must quite simply practice leading. After all, even naturally gifted athletes must practice to compete well. All the training programs and leadership style identifiers are worthless until you step out and test your mettle. Regardless of your current job assignment, there are leadership opportunities all around you. Look in your local community, church, or synagogue for opportunities to lead and serve. Accept a leadership role, steward a project, take actions you think most authentically leader-like, and bring a project to fruition. Then reflect on what you did well and learn where you can improve. Then do it again and again. Bring your beginner's mind to each experience. Engage your learner genes because you have a lot to learn.

You can also practice your leadership skills even when you aren't the actual leader on the project. Consider a project where you wanted the leader position but someone else was selected for it. How you participate, offer ideas, engage in conversations with your colleagues, and use your body language will reveal your innermost feelings about the situation at hand. Remember the cliché, actions speak louder than words. If you are envious or resent that you were not selected to lead the project, your emotional field will belie what you say. People will notice and may project their own interpretations on what they observe.

Employing the gift of introspection, you can take time to sift through your emotions about the situation. You can work through any ego issues that could derail and sabotage your best efforts during the project to better govern your emotions. By understanding yourself and by disciplining your actions (core change practices), you enable yourself to develop an action plan that more closely aligns with your follower role. When you are authentic—whether leading or following—your actions, emotions, and physical presence will coalesce to support your actions.

> *Before you are a leader, success is all about growing yourself.*
> *When you become a leader, success is all about growing others.*
> *—Jack Welch*

Exploring Our Leader Journeys

My personal leadership learning journey started the day I read one single sentence that encapsulated what I have come to believe to be the essence of authentic leadership. It comes from Max DePree's book *Leadership Is an Art:* "In short, the true leader enables his or her followers to realize their full potential." In a momentary flash of brilliant insight, my thinking was forever changed. What did I need to change about me, about my actions to come closer to what I now embraced as the type of leader I wanted to become? Very empowering! I grabbed the brass ring of empowered actions and began to work on me—who I was, who I am, how I show up. It has been a one-step-forward-two-steps-back affair. For every bit of progress, there have been blood, sweat, and tears—of frustration and of joy. I finally realized that my leadership development was in my own hands. My mission, what I really wanted to do with my life, was to help others develop fulfilling lives. Talk about closing the loop!

To make this possible, I knew I needed to help people appreciate the context within which they were living and making their choices. Context is all about how you see the world, hold yourself in relation to what you experience, craft stories to make sense of it all, and then choose your next action. Underlying all of this is the desire to lead a fulfilling life, which is what most people will agree is what they truly want to do (though their definition of fulfilling may differ considerably). The common nugget is the ability to lead, whether it is an external group or just yourself.

To help flesh out the essence of leadership, the opening activity in all of my leadership development workshops is to ask participants to list five people, living or dead, who they believe exemplify the traits, qualities, and attributes of a leader and someone they would willingly follow. That you would follow the person is important. Good and evil play a role here. Throughout time, people have assumed the leadership mantle through fear and coercion. I am making the claim that this is not leadership. It is terrorism. Kill or be killed. The struggle participants have creating this list is palpable. Next I ask participants to list ten traits, qualities, characteristics, and attributes of leadership. Then, I ask them to form small groups and be committed listeners for one another as they each share their lists and make their cases for the qualities they ascribed to leadership. The final task is to agree on the five most important qualities, that absolutely, positively, have to be present for someone in a leadership role, acknowledging up front that there are more than five.

The ensuing conversations are enlightening. The point behind the activity is to strip away the rhetoric, media spin, and other external influences in order to encourage deeper individual thought about what is needed from our leaders. My goal is to stimulate participants to construct their own personal definition of leadership—one they can strive to achieve. I'm told by participants that the exercise has legs. Thinking about what it really takes to lead today and what they want in someone they commit to following can garner lasting insights into leadership.

For the record, the five qualities that epitomize leadership in my mind are 1) being trustworthy in all of my actions; 2) embracing a moral compass predicated on my Judeo-Christian teachings; 3) tapping into the wisdom of my age, experiences, and knowledge to clarify my assessments and inform my actions; 4) having the courage of my convictions when I act; and 5) offering service to others in ways that will help them enjoy purpose-filled, fruitful lives. While far from perfect, these are the principles that I use to guide my daily actions and build relationships.

What qualities epitomize leadership for you? To answer this question, you can start by exploring your vision of yourself as an authentic leader. I've included a Leadership Development Reflection Worksheet at the end of this application to help guide your experience. Remember, introspection's gift is in charge. Take some time to complete the worksheet now.

The last exercise in the worksheet asks you to assess how your own actions stack up against your top-five list. Consider a recent event. Think back to your actions and how you performed. Were your actions consistent with your top-five list? Were you leader-like? Was there a gap between how you took action (your language, your emotional field, your body) and how you believe a leader acts? Listen to your quiet voice as it speaks to your head and your heart, shows you what is missing, and suggests new actions and ways of being. Write down your guiding image of the leader you want to become.

The great leader is seen as servant first.
—Robert Greenleaf

Embodied Leading—Embodied Serving

The influential book *Servant Leadership* by Robert Greenleaf is in my opinion the seminal work on leadership. Its influence has spearheaded a transformational movement uniting the idea of leading with serving others. Seeing yourself as a valuable contributor, as someone who has something to offer others and can therefore lead and be of service, is a mind set. Its seeds germinate early in your life. What mental imagery and beliefs would need to change for you to embrace this idea? How would your language need to change to support you? How might you hold your body differently if you truly believed that you could contribute in a meaningful way to the people in your life? How would you stand? How would you move? How would you show up differently in the relationships you have and what would be different about the conversations you hold?

Think about it. Every encounter you have with others is ripe with possibilities to step outside of yourself, to lead and contribute to their lives, to be of service to them. All you need do is ask, either silently or out loud, the dynamic duo engagement questions already shared: *What do you need? How can I be helpful here?* Each encounter gives you a magical opportunity to bring out the best in someone else and show you genuinely care. The question to consider is, *Who am I being in this moment?* You could also ask, *Who do I need to be to truly be of service to this person?* Even in the most fleeting encounter, sharing a kind word of encouragement and showing interest are acts of service from you to another person.

It is not the size or scope of the project that makes you an authentic leader. It is how you approach people and exert influence that reveals the leader within you. When your emotional field pulses with giving, abundance, caring, and generosity, it is easy to empathize, to unbind yourself from ego, and to look for opportunities to truly serve and contribute. When these elements are missing—when you are trapped in the WIIFM (what's in it for me) mentality—it is harder to serve and contribute. Your belief that something is missing for you stops you cold. How you perceive your own reality informs how you contribute, lead, and serve.

You may find yourself uncomfortable at first as you try out new ways of speaking, listening, and responding. When any discomfort arises consider where it is coming from and what emotion is feeding it power. Is it your fear of changing? Is it a concern about what others might think of your new actions? Is it your wanting something new for yourself without doing the work that bringing about a new you requires? What new distinctions do you need to embrace to diminish your concerns so that the uncomfortable and unfamiliar may become your new friends?

Feeding your budding leadership begins when you take action based on your answers to the questions above. And all you need is a context, a project to lead, so that you can experience yourself in action. I encourage you to start small but meaningful—a cause bigger than yourself that you can really dig your teeth into and that can inspire committed followers.

Community organizations and religious affiliations provide the fertile soil within which you learn how to graciously and generously contribute to and serve others. While these groups provide the outlet, the fundamental building blocks of your ability to be of service actually reside in your own sense of self: your dignity, self-respect, and trustworthiness. My belief is that people are naturally aspirational and naturally generous. They want to better themselves, to learn, to grow, and to develop fully. And they want the same things for other people. When you embody service, you help others achieve and reach their goals, and, more often than not, in the process you achieve your goals as well.

Use the tools you have been learning about. For example, applying the L-E-B Model (Figure 2.2) will foster integrity-based actions. Remember, those are the only behaviors that pull the three domains of action together. Next, pull out the Dance of Effective Change Model (Figure 2.6). Remember that you always start from a centered place. Which of the archetypes will you embody when sharing your vision? How can you offer people who choose to follow your lead a sense of stability even as you weave your story about the vision for a new possible future together? What can you do to create the space for receiving ideas from others so that they embrace your vision and achieve buy-in? What behaviors, actions, and language will you use to support people as they work to bring to life the vision you are describing?

Move to your introspection practice. Keep in mind that your underlying goal is to transform your own leadership capabilities. The project, while important, is serving as the vehicle through which you are accomplishing this goal. Monitor the scope and progress of your project. For example, a project that isn't the right fit, say, if you have chosen a project too small for your commitment, may be revealed in your emotional field when you share your vision for the project's outcome with others; if you aren't excited and engaged, your language and word choices may not resonate with them. Your body may not support you and may appear to others as lack of confidence. When you are invested in the successful outcome of a project your words, energy, and body will stand strong with you.

As you replay events consider how you assess the progress toward the goal in ways that offer you fresh insights to hone your leadership development. When your thinking exposes an issue, embrace this information as a learning opportunity. You can begin to think through ways to handle situations differently, change your actions, behaviors, and language, whatever it will take to continue your leader growth. Who is the person showing up each time to influence, lead, and serve the group? What shifts might you make to deepen your resolve? Where do you experience a disconnect among how you are showing up, your commitment to the project's goals, and your actions? How are your actions honoring yourself? How are your actions honoring others? Take care not to beat yourself up. That misses the point and is counterproductive.

As you work through exercising leadership on this important project, you will begin to notice subtle shifts in your natural way of being. The more you repeat actions that are aligned with the leader you want to become, the more embodied these actions will become. Soon you will naturally be the authentic leader that you are now envisioning.

> *The thing that lies at the foundation of positive change,*
> *the way I see it, is service to a fellow human being.*
> *—Lech Walesa*

Linking Organizations with Leading and Serving

Organizations face their own leadership development challenges because they cultivate their own beliefs about leading, contributing, and serving. And observed actions often speak louder than any words printed on a company document. Embedded in its culture is the day-to-day expression of attitudes, beliefs, moods, and emotions that your company has anointed as acceptable within its walls. Every interaction creates an impression with both customers and employees that eventually becomes a judgment, a mental score card of sorts. Employees are constantly answering the question: *How is it for me?* As individuals make their mental hash marks about how they and others are treated, the culture of the company becomes a composite of those judgments.

Take care! When you join an organization, your own beliefs might get subjugated to the culture that currently permeates in that organization. These actions and behaviors can begin to color your world, becoming the transparent platform of interactions and relationships within your company. When the judgment falls on the positive side, everything is fine. But when the hash marks in the negative column outweigh those on the positive side, your organization's culture begins to decline. Authentic leading and serving can fall victim to apathy, carelessness, and disrespect. This is when employees start to work against each other in very subtle, often imperceptible ways. It can happen slowly over time and in separate departments. Then all of a sudden, your workplace just isn't engaging or productive anymore and serves no one. Employees are numb, just going through the motions. Morale suffers. The downward spiral escalates as these actions continue to feed one another. People do only what is required, nothing more. The negativity takes its toll, eventually impacting customers, sales, and profits.

You have reached a personal tipping point and you will feel it. Your immediate challenge then becomes one of clarifying your own aspirations and coupling these to your current organization. If authentic leading and serving are your priorities, but they are given no more than lip service in the organization, it may be time to consider an exit strategy.

In the final analysis, your ability to lead and be of service reveals the essence of who you are. It embodies a simple truth: we are all experiencing our lives together. Stripped to our core, we are human beings, with strengths and weaknesses, gifts and talents. Not better than someone else, not worse. We have common needs—food, clothing shelter, meaningful work, loving relationships. We don't live in a vacuum: our actions have ramifications on others, both good and bad. Our responsibilities may be different, our education and life adventures diverse. We are each unique versions of God's creation.

A leader is best when people barely know he exists,
when his work is done, his aim fulfilled,
they will say: we did it ourselves.
—*Lao Tzu*

Insights for Action

Leading and serving are rewarding in their own right. Living truthfully in thought, word, and deed, maintaining your integrity in the face of problems, is one of leadership's greatest challenges. Your humanity is front and center in both endeavors. Serving others creates your relationships, and because relationships are not static, you can create, recover, or recreate relationships through collaborative efforts and wise choices. Since the culture of your organization exists in all three domains—language, emotions, and body—you already have an appreciation for how to think about new ways to be.

When you embody leading and serving as your natural way to be, you hold yourself accountable in a different and distinct light. Once these practices are embodied, it becomes very difficult to fall back into your old habits. And if you are not being real, being true to your "self," others will see through your charade quickly. Once lost, it is hard to recover your reputation. That is why self-awareness and self-discipline make up the first practice in the change intelligence factor. When combined with introspection and taking effective actions, the three practices enable you to transcend and to grow outside of your "self" to produce powerful outcomes. The bottom line is this—when you know who you are you can act with confidence.

As you connect to who you are at the deepest level, you will notice even more opportunities to serve. You can think about which actions will best serve the desired outcome and discipline your own contributions along those lines. You become your best doing work that stimulates the mind and also feeds the heart. Your underlying goal is growth: your own and that of others within your sphere of influence. What I am describing is both sustainable and profitable. Many companies have instituted practices that revolve around leadership as service. The return on their investment in their employees speaks volumes: cultivating loyal employees who enjoy their work and serve their customers with pride translates into profitability and prosperity across the board. If you don't currently work for a company like this (and alas, I never did), you can still strive to be like them.

> *If your actions inspire others to dream more,*
> *learn more, do more, and become more,*
> *you are a leader.*
> *—John Quincy Adams*

ACTIVITY: Reflecting on Leadership Development

List five people, living or dead, who you believe epitomize leadership and who you would willingly follow. Then list ten traits, qualities, attributes, and characteristics that you believe leaders must have. Take your time here. Be deliberate with the words and phrases you select. Narrow your list of ten to the top five qualities that must absolutely be present for someone to be a leader in your mind. Compare your two lists. Do the names on your first list exhibit the qualities on your second?

Finally, assess how you stack up against the kind of leaders you admire and want to follow. What traits do you share in common? How can you reinforce those positive traits in your interactions with others? What traits do you lack? Think about ways to add the attributes you lack into your leadership repertoire.

ACTIVITY: Reflecting on Leadership Development / Worksheet

Leadership Development Reflection Worksheet	
List 5 people living or dead who epitomize leadership in your mind.	1. 2. 3. 4. 5.
List 10 traits, qualities, attributes, or characteristics that you believe someone must have to be a leader.	1. 2. 3. 4. 5. 6. 7. 8. 9. 10.
Narrow your list to your top 5 that absolutely, positively have to be present in someone you would willingly follow.	1. 2. 3. 4. 5.
Assess how your own actions stack up against your top 5. Which qualities are strong? Which are weak? Which are missing?	Strong Qualities
	Weak Qualities
	Missing Qualities

ACTIVITY: Organize Your Leader Learning

It is hard to develop your leadership skills without opportunities to practice what you are learning. Here is a worksheet to help you organize your leadership learning goals during your learning project.

Leadership Learning Goals Worksheet	
Project Scope	Describe the project and the desired end goal.
Leader Learning Goal	Choose something like learning how to expand my influence, grow my courage to work outside my comfort zone, challenge my thinking in new more expansive ways, learn how to turn my vision into one others can share.
What language supports his goal?	
What emotional field supports this goal?	
What body attributes support this goal?	
Focus Learning Action 1	Specify an action that you do to develop your leader learning goal.
Focus Learning Action 2	Specify an action that you do to develop your leader learning goal.

4

Your Personal Challenge:
Embrace Personal Transformation

*As human beings, our greatness lies not so much in being able to
remake the world—that is the myth of the atomic age—
as in being able to remake ourselves.*
—Mohandas K. Gandhi

You have reached the end of your reading. You may be asking
yourself, "Now what?" Take heart, this is where the fun begins. You
are now ready to invent, to create the life you really want to be
living.

Conjure up the image of the lobster, crab, or other creature that must
shed its present skeleton in order to grow. Try to picture that
moment of total vulnerability when the animal crawls out of its
shell, defenseless against predators. Personal growth works in much
the same way. Every life is a work in progress. Ask yourself where
is your life going? And is this really where you want to go? Keeping
your head down, existing day-to-day in survival mode is not an
option for a joyful and fulfilling life. For you to grow to your next
stage of development, you must shed your proverbial shell.

Starting with the very essence of who you are now, you can leave
the safety of your comfort zone; accept that you have room to
grow, professionally and personally, and open yourself to new

possibilities. Despite the risks that can leave you feeling vulnerable and unsure, you can choose to welcome new challenges for what they are—opportunities to grow. Personal growth is the antithesis of complacency. It demands courage, resiliency, and just enough dissatisfaction with your current state of affairs to spark your curiosity about what else could be out there.

> *You must be continually learning and growing, exploring how you can become an extra-ordinary person, a supportive partner, and a source of inspiration for others.*
> —*Jane R. Flagello*

Because personal growth is often slow and subtle, it is sometimes hard to recognize your progress. Have you noticed any changes yet? Maybe you are feeling more in control. Perhaps you are noticing that you are managing your emotions more appropriately and effectively when difficult situations arise. Maybe you are taking more time to reflect, thinking through events to discover new possibilities before you act. It could be that your enhanced consciousness is enabling you to generate new behaviors more focused on the specific outcomes you really want.

The philosopher Kierkegaard said that "We all come to earth with sealed orders." Your everyday experiences are actually learning opportunities in disguise. Your only job is to figure out what each problem is trying to teach you, learn the intended lesson, and then move on to the next challenge that comes your way. Alas, the universe has a strange sense of humor. It wants to get your attention, your full attention. When you refuse to learn the lesson before you, it presents itself in more powerful ways. Have you had any close calls lately? Are you ignoring anything in your work and personal life that is clamoring for your attention right now?

The discussion about archetypes in chapter 2 touched on an important consideration, your personal story. Your personal story is like an internal traffic cop, telling you what you can and can't do.

Externally, your personal story is the process of socialization. You are born into a tradition that existed before you arrived. That tradition comprises values and mores that automatically become yours. As you develop, you continue to define yourself through the behaviors, values, and social skills you adopt as well as those you reject.

Internally, you have your own story that connects you to your workplace, community, and family culture. What is it that you tell yourself is true about you? This deeply held, often-invisible narrative informs who you are at a core level. Uncovering the roots of the story behind what you hold to be true about yourself is a first critical growth step because it reveals what you believe possible for yourself as well as what you believe impossible for yourself (your perceived limitations).

For example, a client shared with me the embarrassment he felt when he realized that his present-day attention-seeking actions stemmed from feeling ignored as a child. As one of seven children, the only way he got any attention was to do something over the top. He realized that this was still his modus operandi. Many of his workplace antics were done simply to get attention. And he told me that for the first time in his life, he knew he had a choice to make.

The good news is that you can change your story going forward. Once you recognize that you want your life to be different—and you accept the challenge to make it happen—your experiences begin to take on a new dimension of clarity. The benefit of transformational learning is that it allows you to shift your story. You can let go of those aspects holding you back and begin to solidify parts of the story that enable your success. You can change what you are doing to create better alignment of actions to outcomes. You begin transforming yourself, utilizing your talents, and maximizing your potential in the service of others. In essence, you move up Maslow's Hierarchy of Needs toward the highest level of self-actualization.

Working within more organic and human dimensions, the three practices that constitute the change intelligence factor—exerting personal discipline, thinking things through, and taking more effective actions—generate a level of transformational learning that actually supports sustainable change. You begin to live "at choice." You embrace living more consciously. You realize that only the relationships you create and hold with others have any real value. Stuff is well, just stuff. Your capabilities expand as you apply new interpretations to the significant experiences in your life. Through conscious actions, you generate a new, more cohesive self as you become ever more capable. As you evolve, you can appreciate your humanness and embrace the unique contribution you can make in the world around you. We are on this earth to live and to grow and to love and to learn. In the end, we all go out as we came in, with nothing, but we leave behind the lives we've been able to touch. I wish you the very best in your journey toward extra-ordinary.

The future belongs to those individuals who are capable of continuous personal learning and development; who are self-motivated, self-led, and self-managed; who see themselves as full contributing partners in an ongoing drama called work, called life.
—*Jane R. Flagello*

ACTIVITY: Mastering Extra-Ordinary Action Map

To commit to a new direction for your personal and professional life is exciting. It can also be overwhelming. Since I know that you can't do everything all at once, the worksheet below is one that my clients have found to be helpful.

Your developing change intelligence is all the fuel you need to power your travels. You are designing a map of the territory—where you want to go. With any journey you need to know what to pack. In this instance, you are packing for both your professional as well as your personal growth. Get a small journal to track your results. Record your progress, acknowledge your victories, and make notes along the way.

ACTIVITY: Mastering Extra-Ordinary Action Map

The first step is to clarify the new path and new destination. In the second step, you define home base—those beliefs and values that will allow you to stand strong. Your home base serves as your unswerving action platform. And in steps three, four, and five, you assess your behaviors from three perspectives: behaviors that are working well for you and that you want to continue, behaviors that you want to change or stop completely because they no longer serve you, and finally new behaviors that you need to start. For example, with your professional goal in mind, what is currently working that you plan to continue? What do you need to change? What do you need to start? Do the same for your personal growth goal and that's six new targeted action initiatives each month—three targeted to your professional goal and three to your personal growth goal. As you identify each behavior, the specific actions you need to take in each category will become clear.

1. **Describe Your New Territory**: Identify two goals—one personal and one professional—that you want to achieve in the next year that you believe will support your journey toward becoming extra-ordinary.

2. **Define Your Home Base**: Identify up to five important beliefs and values that you hold dear and that are non-negotiable for you. These are areas where you clearly draw your line in the sand and that you do not cross.

3. **Continue:** Think about current behaviors and actions you take that produce solid results for you. They feel natural, and your performance is smooth and easy. Identify these areas as behaviors and actions that you want to continue doing, and perhaps even strengthen.

4. **Change:** Consider areas where your behaviors are not producing the results you want. These are actions that diminish your effectiveness or conflict with your core values that you need to change. These can also be behaviors that you need to totally stop doing. What's really happening? What's missing? Think about the small lies you tell yourself that deep in your heart you know are untrue. What behaviors might produce better results for you? If you are unsure, ask people who will truthfully offer insights and suggestions for changes that will increase your effectiveness. After each behavior, list two specific actions that will help you change these behaviors.

5. **Start:** Identify new behaviors and practices that will better serve you as you move toward the personal and professional life you really want to be yours. Use the tools, techniques, models, and strategies you have been learning about in this book. Start interacting in ways that will increase the space of empowered actions.

Influential Readings

Here is a list of books and articles that have been significant in my learning. Some are directly mentioned in *The Change Intelligence Factor: Mastering the Promise of Extra-Ordinary,* while others are included because of the influence these authors had in my thinking, my learning, my coaching, and my personal growth. Enjoy!

Argyris, C., and D. Schon. 1974. *Theory in Practice: Increasing Professional Effectiveness.* San Francisco: Jossey-Bass.

Austin, J. L. 1973. *How to Do Things with Words.* 2nd ed. Cambridge, MA: Harvard University Press.

Block, P. 2008. *Community: The Structure of Belonging.* San Francisco: Berrett-Koehler.

———. 2002. *The Answer to How Is Yes: Acting on What Matters.* San Francisco: Berrett-Koehler.

Brothers, C. 2005. *Language and the Pursuit of Happiness: A New Foundation for Designing Your Life, Your Relationships, and Your Results.* Naples, FL: New Possibilities Press.

Bryner, A., and D. Markova. 1996. *An Unused Intelligence: Physical Thinking for 21st Century Leadership.* Berkeley, CA: Conari Press.

Budd, M., and I. Rothstein. 2000. *You Are What You Say: A Harvard Doctor's Six-Step Program for Transforming Stress Through the Power of Language.* New York: Crown.

Collins, J. 2002. *Good to Great: Why Some Companies Make the Leap and Others Don't.* New York: HarperCollins.

Courcy, C. 2012. *Save Your Inner Tortoise!* Bloomington, IN: Balboa Press.

Covey, S. R. 2004. *The 8th Habit.* New York: Free Press.

———. 1989. *7 Habits of Highly Effective People.* New York: Simon & Schuster.

Csikszentmihalyi, M. 1993. *The Evolving Self: A Psychology for the Third Millennium.* New York: HarperCollins.

DePree, M. 1989. *Leadership Is an Art*. New York: Doubleday.

Erhard, W., M. C. Jensen, and K. L. Granger. 2010. "Creating Leaders: An Ontological/Phenomonological Model," Harvard Business School NOM Unit Working Paper No.11-037, Barbados Group Working Paper No. 10-10, and Simon School Working Paper Series No. FR-10-30; available online at http://ssrn.com/abstract=1681682.

Flores, F., and R. Solomon. 2001. *Building Trust*. New York: Oxford University Press.

Gallwey, W. T. 2000. *The Inner Game of Work*. New York: Random House.

Goleman, D. 1998. *Working with Emotional Intelligence*. New York: Bantam.

———. 1995. *Emotional Intelligence: Why It Can Matter More Than IQ*. New York: Bantam.

Greenleaf, R. 1997. *Servant Leadership: A Journey into the Nature of Legitimate Power and Greatness*. New York: Paulist Press.

Heckler, R. S. 1997. *Holding the Center: Sanctuary in a Time of Confusion*. Berkeley, CA, Frog.

———. 1993. *The Anatomy of Change: A Way to Move Through Life's Transitions*. Berkeley, CA: North Atlantic Books.

Kegan, R., and L. L. Lahey. 2009. *Immunity to Change: How to Overcome It and Unlock Potential in Yourself and Your Organization*. Cambridge, MA: Harvard University Press.

LeDoux, J. E. 2000. "Emotion Circuits in the Brain," in *Annual Review of Neuroscience* 23: 155–84.

Leonard, G. 1991. *Mastery: The Keys to Success and Long-Term Fulfillment*. New York: Penguin.

Leonard, G., and M. Murphy. 1995. *The Life We Are Given: A Long-Term Program for Realizing the Potential of Body, Mind, Heart, and Soul*. New York: Penguin.

Mayer, J., and P. Salovey. 1990. "Emotional Intelligence," in *Imagination, Cognition, and Personality* 9: 185–211.

Olalla, J. 2000. *Proceedings of Newfield Network Coaching for Personal and Professional Mastery Conference*, March 27. Alexandria, VA: Newfield Network, Inc.

Patterson, K., J. Grenny, D. Maxfield, R. McMillan, and A. Switzler. 2008. *Influencer: The Power to Change Anything.* New York: McGraw-Hill.

Ruiz, D. M. 1997. *The Four Agreements.* San Rafael, CA: Amber-Allen.

Sieler, A. 2003. *Coaching to the Human Soul: Ontological Coaching and Deep Change*, vol. 1. Blackburn, Australia: Newfield Australia.

Spinosa, C., F. Flores, and H. Dreyfus. 1997. *Disclosing New Worlds.* Cambridge, MA: MIT Press.

Wheatley, M. 2002. *Turning to One Another: Simple Conversations to Restore Hope to the Future.* San Francisco: Berrett-Koehler.

Wilbur, K. 1996. *A Brief History of Everything.* Boston: Shambhala.

Winograd, T., and F. Flores. 1986. *Understanding Computers and Cognition: A New Foundation for Design.* Norwood, NJ: Ablex.

Zander, B., and R. Zander. 2000. *The Art of Possibility.* Cambridge, MA: Harvard Business School Press.

Acknowledgments

The learning and growth that I experienced as a result of my ontological coaching program through The Newfield Network and the insights offered by Julio Olalla, its founder, challenged my thinking and gave birth to this book. The people at Newfield are amazing. I am very grateful to Newfield for giving me permission to reference the concepts I learned in its program and apply them in my own unique way. Newfield's teachings offer organizations a different way to think through the challenges confronting them and to bring about new possibilities. I am so thankful that my own journey led me to its doorstep: I strongly encourage you to investigate Newfield's programs and offerings at www.newfieldnetwork.com.

My previous book, *The Savvy Manager: 5 Skills That Drive Optimal Performance,* co-authored with Dr. Sandra Dugas and published by ASTD Press (2009), also played a role in shaping the concepts presented here.

I want to thank Ivan Farber who was my "fresh pair of eyes" and offered wonderful insights on what worked and where I needed to do some more work.

Thanks to Cat Russo, Jacki Edlund-Braun, Debra Deysher, and everyone at TPH for their hard work and support in helping to bring this book to the public. I could not have done this without all of you, and I am grateful that you showed up at just the right time. Magic!

And finally, thank you to my husband, John, who again gave his love and support throughout this writing.

About the Author

Jane R. Flagello devotes her time and attention to motivational speaking, training, writing, and coaching people in organizations through change initiatives to produce extra-ordinary results.

Serving the business and education community for more than 40 years, Jane embraces the idea people have the ability to create great places to work, places that feed the creative spirit and ignite the innovative talents so necessary today.

With a doctorate in adult learning and certification as an ontological coach, Jane helps people figure out what their gifts and talents are and shows them how to best leverage these talents to generate a rich and rewarding life.

Jane resides in Williamsburg, Virginia.

Learn more about Jane and her work on change intelligence at www.changeintelligence.net.

About TPH

You've got ideas. You have a proven track record. You want to share your success. But, how? We can help.

Who We Are

We are experienced training & development publishers, who have spent more than 30 years working in the workplace, learning & development industry. We have the expertise and professional contacts that can take your winning ideas and turn them into respected, go-to training & development resources.

What We Do

We publish solid, academically-worthy training & development content through any and all of the following steps:

1. Proposal review

2. Content editing

3. Book layout and design

4. Production—both print and electronic books

5. Subsidiary rights facilitation

How to Get Started

Submit your proposal to
http://www.trainerspublishinghouse.com/contact-us.html
and we'll be in touch to get the ball rolling!